Curriculum in Early Education

Carol Gestwicki

THOMSON

™

DELMAR LEARNING

Australia • Canada • Mexico • Singapore • Spain • United Kingdom • United States

NOTICE TO THE READER

The authors and Thomson Delmar Learning affirm that the Web site URLs referenced herein were accurate at the time of printing. However, due to the fluid nature of the Internet, we cannot guarantee their accuracy for the life of the edition.

Join us on the web at
EarlyChildEd.delmar.com

TABLE OF CONTENTS

This tool was developed to help you, the budding teacher and/or childcare provider, as you move into your first classroom. The editors at Thomson Delmar Learning encourage and appreciate your feedback on this or any of our other products. Go to http://www.earlychilded. delmar.com and click on the "Professional Enhancement series feedback" link to let us know what you think.

INTRODUCTION

Throughout a college preparation program to become an early childhood educator, students take many courses and read many textbooks. Their knowledge grows, as they accumulate ideas from lectures, reading, experiences, and discussions. When they finish their coursework, graduate, and move into their first teaching positions, students often leave behind some of the books they have used. The hope is, however, that they will take with them the important ideas from their classes and books as they begin their own professional practice.

More experienced colleagues or mentors sometimes support teachers in their first teaching positions, helping them make the transition from college classroom to being responsible for a group of young children. Other times, new teachers are left to travel their own paths, relying on their own resources. Whatever your situation, this professional enhancement guide is designed to provide reminders of what you have learned, as well as resources to help you make sense of and apply that knowledge.

Teachers of young children are under great pressure today. From families, there are often demands for support in their difficult tasks of child-rearing in today's fast-paced and changing world. Some families become so overwhelmed with the tasks of parenting that they seem to leave too much responsibility on the shoulders of teachers and caregivers. From administrators and institutions, expectations sometimes seem overwhelming. Teachers are being held accountable for children's learning in ways unprecedented in even the recent past. Public scrutiny has led to insistence on teaching practices that may seem contrary to the best interests of children or their teachers. New teachers may find themselves caught between the realities of the schools or centers where they find themselves and their own philosophies and ideals of working with children. When faced with such dilemmas, it is important for these individuals to fall back and reflect on what they know of best practices, renewing their professional determination to make appropriate decisions for children.

These books provide similar tools for that reflection:

- Tips for getting off to a great start in your new environment

- Information about typical developmental patterns of children from birth through school age

- Suggestions for materials that promote development for children from infancy through the primary grades

- Tools to assist teachers in observing children and gathering data to help set appropriate goals for individual children

- Guides for planning appropriate classroom experiences and sample lesson plans

- Tips for introducing children to the joys of literacy

- A summary of the key ideas about developmentally appropriate practice, the process of decision-making that allows teachers to provide optimum environments for children from birth through school age

- Professional development resources for teachers

- Ideas of where you can access lists of other resources

- Case studies of relevant, realistic situations you may face, as well as best practices for successfully navigating them

- Insight into issues and trends facing early childhood educators today

Becoming a teacher is a process of continuing to grow, learn, reflect, and discover through experience. These resources will help you along your way. Good luck on your journey!

REFLECTIONS FOR GROWING TEACHERS

Teachers spend most of their time working with young children and their families. During the day, questions and concerns arise and decisions must be made, meaning teachers must always be reflective about their work. Too often, teachers believe they are too busy to spend time thinking, but experienced professional teachers know that reflection sustains their best work. Growing teachers need to regularly take time to consider the questions and concerns that arise from their practice. Some teachers use journals to keep track of the process.

Use these questions to begin your reflection and then add to them with questions from your own experience. Remember, these are not questions to be answered once and forgotten, come back to them often.

QUESTIONS FOR REFLECTION

This day would have been better if_____

_____

_____.

I think I need to know more about _____

_____

_____.

One new thing I think I'll try this week is _____

_____

_____

The highlight of this week was _____

_____

_____

The observations this week made me think more about _____

_____

_____

I think my favorite creative activity this year was _____

_____

_____

One area where my teaching is changing is _____

_____

_____

One area where my teaching needs to change is _____

_____

_____

I just don't understand why _____

_____

_____

I loved my job this week when _____

_____

_____

I hated my job this week when _____

_____

_____

One thing I can try to make better next week is _____

_____

_____

The funniest thing I heard a child say this week was _____

_____

_____.

The family member I feel most comfortable with is _____

_____

_____.

And I think the reason for that is _____

_____

_____.

The family member I feel least comfortable with is _____

_____

_____.

And I think the reason for that is _____

_____

_____.

The biggest gains in learning have been made by _____

_____

_____.

And I think that this is because _____

_____

_____.

I'm working on a bad habit of _____

_____

_____.

Has my attitude about teaching changed this year? Why? _____

_____

_____.

What have I done lately to spark the children's imagination and creativity? ____

_____

_____.

One quote that I like to keep in mind is _____

_____

_____.

Dealing with _____ is the most difficult thing I had to face recently because _____

_____

_____.

My teaching style has been most influenced by _____

_____

_____.

In thinking more about Developmentally Appropriate Practice in my curriculum,
I believe _____

_____

_____.

If I were going to advise a new teacher, the most helpful piece of advice would be

_____

_____.

I've been trying to facilitate friendships among the children by _____

_____

_____.

I really need to start_____

_____

_____.

I used to _____ but now I _____

_____

_____.

The child who has helped me learn the most is _____. I learned _____

_____

_____.

I've grown in my communication by _____

_____

_____.

The best thing I've learned by observing is _____
_____
_____.

I still don't understand why _____
_____
_____.

One mistake I used to make that I don't make any longer is _____
_____
_____.

When next year starts, one thing I will do more of is _____
_____
_____.

When next year starts, one thing I won't do is _____
_____
_____.

One way I can help my children feel more competent is _____
_____
_____.

Something I enjoy that I could share with my class is _____
_____
_____.

When children have difficulty sharing, I _____
_____
_____
_____
_____.

Adapted from Nilsen, B.A., *Week by Week: Documenting the Development of Young Children,* (3rd ed.), published by Thomson Delmar Learning.

TIPS FOR SUCCESS

Remember that you are a role model for the children. They are constantly watching how you dress, what you say, and what you do. Also, as parents perceive a teacher's professionalism, they are often more responsive to communication and partnership.

BE A PROFESSIONAL

- Dress conservatively and follow your employer's clothing expectations (which could include wearing closed-toe shoes to be safe and active with children and wearing clean, modest, and comfortable clothing).

- Be prepared and on time.

- Avoid excessive absences.

- Use appropriate language with children and adults.

- Be positive when talking to parents and show that you are forming a positive relationship with their child and wanting to form a partnership with the family. "Catch children doing something right" and share those accomplishments with parents. Discuss challenges you have with children after you have established trust with the parents.

BE A TEAM PLAYER

- Rely on team members to help you learn the parameters of your new position.

- Don't be afraid to ask questions or for guidance from teammates.

- Show your support and be responsible.

- Step in to do your share of the work; don't expect others to clean up after you.

- Assist others whenever possible.

- Respect others' ideas and avoid telling them how to do things.

- Strive to balance your ability to make decisions with following the lead of others.

LEARN ABOUT CHILDREN

- Be aware of their development physically, socially, emotionally, and cognitively.

- Assess children's development and plan curriculum that will enhance that development.

- Be aware that children will test you! (Children, especially school age, expect that you don't know the rules and may try to convince you to let them do things that were not previously allowed.)

- Never hesitate to double-check something with teammates when in doubt.

- Use positive guidance techniques with children.

GUIDANCE TECHNIQUES FOR GAINING CHILDREN'S COOPERATION

Myriad techniques are available to help children cooperate. Children need respectful reminders of expectations and adult support to perform in a way that meets those expectations. Be sure that your expectations are age appropriate and individually appropriate. These techniques are more preventive in nature.

- Use positive phrases and state exactly what you expect children to do. "Stand by the door" is more effective than "Don't go outside until everyone is ready."

- Avoid "no" and "don't." Be clear about what it is you want children to do, not what you don't want them to do.

- Sequence directions using "When-then." For example, "When things are put away where they belong, then we can go outside."

- ■ Stay close. Merely standing near children can be enough to help them manage behavior. Be aware, however, that if you are talking to another adult, children may act out because they know they do not have your attention.

- ■ Offer sufficient and appropriate choices. Children need a variety of activities that interest them and that will create opportunities for success.

Create a schedule that balances children's activity with quieter periods to help children retain control.

GETTING STARTED

When starting in a new position working with children, there is always an array of information to learn. Use this fill-in-the blank section to customize this resource book to your specific environment.

What are the school's or center's hours of operation? .

On school days: _____

_____

_____

On vacation days: _____

_____

_____

What is the basic daily schedule and what are my responsibilities during each time segment?

_____

_____

_____

_____

_____

_____

_____

What are the procedures for checking children in and out of the program?

_____

_____

_____

_____

Do I call if I have to be absent? Who is my contact?

Name:_____

Phone Number: _____

What is the dress code for employees?

_____

_____

_____

For what basic health and safety practices will I be responsible? Where are the materials stored for this? (Bleach, gloves, etc.)

Sanitizing tables: _____

_____

_____

_____

Cleaning and maintaining equipment and materials: _____

_____

_____

_____

What are the emergency procedures?

Mildly injured child: _____

_____

_____

_____

_____

Earthquake/Tornado: _____

_____

_____

_____

_____

Fire: _____

_____

_____

_____

_____

First Aid:_____

_____

_____

_____

Other:_____

_____

_____

_____

DEVELOPMENTAL MILESTONES BY AGE

Whether you are working with infants, toddlers, preschoolers, or primary-aged children, a teacher's first requirement is to know how children develop and learn. In your college program, you no doubt studied child development. The following is a shortened version of the universal steps most children go through as they develop. Some children will move easily from one step to another, whereas other children move forward in one area but lag behind in others. Use these milestones as a guide for arranging an environment or planning activities in your room.

Child's Name _____   Age _____
Observer _____   Date _____

DEVELOPMENTAL CHECKLIST

By Six Months: Does the child . . .	Yes	No	Sometimes
Show continued gains in height, weight, and head circumference?			
Reach for toys or objects when they are presented?			
Begin to roll from stomach to back?			
Sit with minimal support?			
Transfer objects from one hand to the other?			
Raise up on arms, lifting head and chest, when placed on stomach?			
Babble, coo, and imitate sounds?			
Turn to locate the source of a sound?			
Focus on an object and follow its movement vertically and horizontally?			

Does the child . . . , continued	Yes	No	Sometimes
Exhibit a blink reflex?			
Enjoy being held and cuddled?			
Recognize and respond to familiar faces?			
Begin sleeping six to eight hours through the night?			
Suck vigorously when it is time to eat?			
Enjoy playing in water during bath time?			

DEVELOPMENTAL ALERTS

Check with a health care provider or early childhood specialist if, by one month of age, the infant *does not*

- show alarm or "startle" responses to loud noise.

- suck and swallow with ease.

- show gains in height, weight, and head circumference.

- grasp with equal strength with both hands.

- make eye-to-eye contact when awake and being held.

- become quiet soon after being picked up.

- roll head from side to side when placed on stomach.

- express needs and emotions with cries and patterns of vocalizations that can be distinguished from one another.

- stop crying when picked up and held.

DEVELOPMENTAL ALERTS

Check with a health care provider or early childhood specialist if, by four months of age, the infant *does not*

- continue to show steady increases in height, weight, and head circumference.

- smile in response to the smiles of others (the social smile is a significant developmental milestone).

- follow a moving object with eyes focusing together.

- bring hands together over midchest.
- turn head to locate sounds.
- begin to raise head and upper body when placed on stomach.
- reach for objects or familiar persons.

Child's Name _____   Age _____
Observer _____   Date _____

DEVELOPMENTAL CHECKLIST

By 12 Months:	Yes	No	Sometimes
Does the child . . .			
Walk with assistance?			
Roll a ball in imitation of an adult?			
Pick objects up with thumb and forefinger?			
Transfer objects from one hand to the other?			
Pick up dropped toys?			
Look directly at the adult's face?			
Imitate gestures: peek-a-boo, bye-bye, patty-cake?			
Find object hidden under a cup?			
Feed self crackers (munching, not sucking on them)?			
Hold cup with two hands; drink with assistance?			
Smile spontaneously?			
Pay attention to own name?			
Respond to "no"?			
Respond differently to strangers and familiar persons?			
Respond differently to sounds: vacuum, phone, door?			
Look at the person who speaks to him or her?			
Respond to simple directions accompanied by gestures?			
Make several consonant–vowel combination sounds?			
Vocalize back to the person who has talked to him or her?			
Use intonation patterns that sound like scolding, asking, exclaiming?			
Say "da-da" or "ma-ma"?			

DEVELOPMENTAL ALERTS

Check with a health care provider or early childhood specialist if, by 12 months of age, the infant *does not*

- blink when fast-moving objects approach the eyes.

- begin to cut teeth.

- imitate simple sounds.

- follow simple verbal requests: *come, bye-bye.*

- pull self to a standing position.

Child's Name _____   Age _____

Observer _____   Date _____

DEVELOPMENTAL CHECKLIST

By Two Years:	Yes	No	Sometimes
Does the child . . .			
Walk alone?			
Bend over and pick up a toy without falling over?			
Seat self in child-size chair? Walk up and down stairs with assistance?			
Place several rings on a stick?			
Place five pegs in a pegboard?			
Turn pages two or three at a time?			
Scribble?			
Follow one-step direction involving something familiar: "Give me _____." "Show me _____." "Get a _____."?			
Match familiar objects?			
Use a spoon with some spilling?			
Drink from a cup holding it with one hand, unassisted?			
Chew food?			
Take off coat, shoe, sock?			
Zip and unzip large zipper?			
Recognize self in a mirror or picture?			
Refer to self by name?			

Does the child . . . , continued	Yes	No	Sometimes
Imitate adult behaviors in play—for example, feeds "baby"?			
Help put things away?			
Respond to specific words by showing what was named: toy, pet, family member?			
Ask for desired items by name: (cookie)?			
Answer with name of object when asked "What's that"?			
Make some two-word statements: "Daddy bye-bye"?			

DEVELOPMENTAL ALERTS

Check with a health care provider or early childhood specialist if, by 24 months of age, the child *does not*

- attempt to talk or repeat words.

- understand some new words.

- respond to simple questions with "yes" or "no."

- walk alone (or with very little help).

- exhibit a variety of emotions: anger, delight, fear.

- show interest in pictures.

- recognize self in mirror.

- attempt self-feeding: hold own cup to mouth and drink.

Child's Name _____   Age _____
Observer _____   Date _____

DEVELOPMENTAL CHECKLIST

By Three Years:	Yes	No	Sometimes
Does the child . . .			
Run well in a forward direction?			
Jump in place, two feet together?			
Walk on tiptoe?			
Throw a ball (but without direction or aim)?			
Kick a ball forward?			

Does the child . . . , continued	Yes	No	Sometimes
String four large beads?			
Turn pages in book singly?			
Hold a crayon: imitate circular, vertical, horizontal strokes?			
Match shapes?			
Demonstrate number concepts of 1 and 2? (Can select 1 or 2; can tell if one or two objects.)			
Use a spoon without spilling?			
Drink from a straw?			
Put on and take off coat?			
Wash and dry hands with some assistance?			
Watch other children; play near them; sometimes join in their play?			
Defend own possessions?			
Use symbols in play—for example, tin pan on head becomes helmet and crate becomes a spaceship?			
Respond to "Put _____ in the box," "Take the _____ out of the box"?			
Select correct item on request: big versus little; one versus two?			
Identify objects by their use: show own shoe when asked, "What do you wear on your feet?"			
Ask questions?			
Tell about something with functional phrases that carry meaning: "Daddy go airplane." "Me hungry now"?			

DEVELOPMENTAL ALERTS

Check with a health care provider or early childhood specialist if, by the third birthday, the child *does not*

- eat a fairly well-rounded diet, even though amounts are limited.

- walk confidently with few stumbles or falls; climb steps with help.

- avoid bumping into objects.

- carry out simple, two-step directions: "Come to Daddy and bring your book"; express desires; ask questions.

- point to and name familiar objects; use two- or three-word sentences.

- enjoy being read to.

- show interest in playing with other children: watching, perhaps imitating.

- indicate a beginning interest in toilet training.

- sort familiar objects according to a single characteristic, such as type, color, or size.

Child's Name _____   Age _____

Observer _____   Date _____

DEVELOPMENTAL CHECKLIST

By Four Years:	Yes	No	Sometimes
Does the child ...			
Walk on a line?			
Balance on one foot briefly? Hop on one foot?			
Jump over an object 6 inches high and land on both feet together?			
Throw ball with direction?			
Copy circles and Xs?			
Match six colors?			
Count to 5?			
Pour well from a pitcher? Spread butter or jam with knife?			
Button, unbutton large buttons?			
Know own sex, age, and last name?			
Use toilet independently and reliably?			
Wash and dry hands unassisted?			
Listen to stories for at least five minutes?			
Draw head of person and at least one other body part?			
Play with other children?			
Share, take turns (with some assistance)?			
Engage in dramatic and pretend play?			
Respond appropriately to "Put it beside," "Put it under"?			
Respond to two-step directions: "Give me the sweater and put the shoe on the floor"?			

Does the child . . . , continued	Yes	No	Sometimes
Respond by selecting the correct object—for example, hard versus soft object?			
Answer "if," "what," and "when" questions?			
Answer questions about function: "What are books for"?			

DEVELOPMENTAL ALERTS

Check with a health care provider or early childhood specialist if, by the fourth birthday, the child *does not*

- have intelligible speech most of the time; have children's hearing checked if there is any reason for concern.

- understand and follow simple commands and directions.

- state own name and age.

- enjoy playing near or with other children.

- use three- to four-word sentences.

- ask questions.

- stay with an activity for three or four minutes; play alone several minutes at a time.

- jump in place without falling.

- balance on one foot, at least briefly.

- help with dressing self.

FIVE- TO SEVEN-YEAR-OLDS

Five- to seven-year old children

- are more independent of parents and are able to take care of their own physical needs.

- rely upon their peer group for self-esteem and have two or three best friends.

- learn to share, take turns, and participate in group games.

- are eager to learn and succeed in school.

- have a sense of duty and develop a conscience.

- are less aggressive and resolve conflicts with words.

- begin to see others' points of view.
- can sustain interest for long periods of time.
- can remember and relate past events.
- have good muscle control and can manage simple tools.
- have a high energy level.

Child's Name _____   Age _____
Observer _____   Date _____

DEVELOPMENTAL CHECKLIST

By Five Years:	Yes	No	Sometimes
Does the child . . .			
Walk backward, heel to toe?			
Walk up and down stairs, alternating feet?			
Cut on line with scissors?			
Print some letters?			
Point to and name three shapes?			
Group common related objects: shoe, sock, and foot; apple, orange, and plum?			
Demonstrate number concepts to 4 or 5?			
Cut food with a knife: celery, sandwich?			
Lace shoes?			
Read from story picture book—in other words, tell story by looking at pictures?			
Draw a person with three to six body parts?			
Play and interact with other children; engage in dramatic play that is close to reality?			
Build complex structures with blocks or other building materials?			
Respond to simple three-step directions: "Give me the pencil, put the book on the table, and hold the comb in your hand"?			
Respond correctly when asked to show a penny, nickel, and dime?			
Ask "How" questions?			
Respond verbally to "Hi" and "How are you"?			
Tell about events using past and future tenses?			
Use conjunctions to string words and phrases together—for example, "I saw a bear and a zebra and a giraffe at the zoo"?			

DEVELOPMENTAL ALERTS

Check with a health care provider or early childhood specialist if, by the fifth birthday, the child *does not*

- state own name in full.

- recognize simple shapes: circle, square, triangle.

- catch a large ball when bounced (have child's vision checked).

- speak so as to be understood by strangers (have child's hearing checked).

- have good control of posture and movement.

- hop on one foot.

- appear interested in, and responsive to, surroundings.

- respond to statements without constantly asking to have them repeated.

- dress self with minimal adult assistance; manage buttons, zippers.

- take care of own toilet needs; have good bowel and bladder control with infrequent accidents.

Child's Name _____   Age _____
Observer _____   Date _____

DEVELOPMENTAL CHECKLIST

By Six Years:	Yes	No	Sometimes
Does the child . . .			
Walk across a balance beam?			
Skip with alternating feet?			
Hop for several seconds on one foot?			
Cut out simple shapes?			
Copy own first name?			
Show well-established handedness; demonstrate consistent right- or left-handedness?			
Sort objects on one or more dimensions: color, shape, or function?			

Does the child . . . , continued	Yes	No	Sometimes
Name most letters and numerals?			
Count by rote to 10; know what number comes next?			
Dress self completely; tie bows?			
Brush teeth unassisted?			
Have some concept of clock time in relation to daily schedule?			
Cross street safely?			
Draw a person with head, trunk, legs, arms, and features; often add clothing details?			
Play simple board games?			
Engage in cooperative play with other children, involving group decisions, role assignments, and rule observance?			
Use construction toys, such as Legos and blocks, to make recognizable structures?			
Do 15-piece puzzles?			
Use all grammatical structures: pronouns, plurals, verb tenses, conjunctions?			
Use complex sentences: carry on conversations?			

DEVELOPMENTAL ALERTS

Check with a health care provider or early childhood specialist if, by the sixth birthday, the child *does not*

- alternate feet when walking up and down stairs.

- speak in a moderate voice; neither too loud, too soft, too high, too low.

- follow simple directions in stated order: "Please go to the cupboard, get a cup, and bring it to me.

- use four to five words in acceptable sentence structure.

- cut on a line with scissors.

- sit still and listen to an entire short story (five to seven minutes).

- maintain eye contact when spoken to (unless this is a cultural taboo).

- play well with other children.

- perform most self-grooming tasks independently: brush teeth, wash hands and face.

Child's Name _____	Age _____
Observer _____	Date _____

DEVELOPMENTAL CHECKLIST

By Seven Years:	Yes	No	Sometimes
Does the child . . .			
Concentrate on completing puzzles and board games?			
Ask many questions?			
Use correct verb tenses, word order, and sentence structure in conversation?			
Correctly identify right- and left hands?			
Make friends easily?			
Show some control of anger, using words instead of physical aggression?			
Participate in play that requires teamwork and rule observance?			
Seek adult approval for efforts?			
Enjoy reading and being read to?			
Use pencil to write words and numbers?			
Sleep undisturbed through the night?			
Catch a tennis ball, walk across the balance beam, hit a ball with a bat?			
Plan and carry out simple projects with minimal adult help?			
Tie own shoes?			
Draw pictures with greater detail and sense of proportion?			
Care for own personal needs with some adult supervision? Wash hands? Brush teeth? Use toilet? Dress self?			
Show some understanding of cause-and-effect concepts?			

DEVELOPMENTAL ALERTS

Check with a health care provider or early childhood specialist if, by the seventh birthday, the child *does not*

- show signs of ongoing growth: increasing height and weight and continuing motor development, such as running, jumping, balancing.

- show some interest in reading and trying to reproduce letters, especially own name.

- follow simple, multiple-step directions: "Finish your book, put it on the shelf, and then get your coat on."

- follow through with instructions and complete simple tasks: putting dishes in the sink, picking up clothes, finishing a puzzle. *Note:* All children forget. Task incompletion is not a problem unless a child *repeatedly* leaves tasks unfinished.

- begin to develop alternatives to excessive use of inappropriate behaviors in order to get own way.

- develop a steady decrease in tension-type behaviors that may have developed with starting school: repeated grimacing or facial tics; eye twitching; grinding teeth; regressive soiling or wetting; frequent stomachaches; refusing to go to school.

EIGHT- TO TEN-YEAR-OLDS

Eight- to ten-year-olds

- need parental guidance and support for school achievement.

- compete with others.

- have pronounced gender differences in interests and form same gender cliques.

- spend a lot of time in physical game playing.

- are aware of the importance of academic achievement.

- begin to develop moral values and make value judgments about own behavior.

- are aware of the importance of belonging.

- conform to strong gender roles.

- begin to think logically and to understand cause and effect.

- use language to communicate ideas and can use abstract words.

- can read but ability varies.

- realize importance of physical skills in determining status among peers.

Child's Name _____   Age _____
Observer _____   Date _____

DEVELOPMENTAL CHECKLIST

By Eight and Nine Years:	Yes	No	Sometimes
Does the child . . .			
Have energy to play, continue growing with few illnesses?			
Use pencil in a deliberate and controlled manner?			
Express relatively complex thoughts in a clear and logical fashion?			
Carry out multiple four- to five-step instructions?			
Become less easily frustrated with own performance?			
Interact and play cooperatively with other children?			
Show interest in creative expression—telling stories, jokes, writing, drawing, singing?			
Use eating utensils with ease?			
Have a good appetite? Show interest in trying new foods?			
Know how to tell time?			
Have control of bowel and bladder functions?			
Participate in some group activities—games, sports, plays?			
Want to go to school? Seem disappointed if must miss a day?			
Demonstrate beginning skills in reading, writing, and math?			
Accept responsibility and complete work independently?			
Handle stressful situations without becoming overly upset?			

DEVELOPMENTAL ALERTS

Check with a health care provider or early childhood specialist if, by the eighth birthday, the child *does not*

- attend to the task at hand; show longer periods of sitting quietly, listening, and responding appropriately.

- follow through on simple instructions.

- go to school willingly most days (of concern are excessive complaints about stomachaches or headaches when getting ready for school).

- make friends (observe closely to see if the child plays alone most of the time or withdraws consistently from contact with other children).

- sleep soundly most nights (frequent and recurring nightmares or bad dreams are usually at a minimum at this age).

- seem to see or hear adequately at times (squints, rubs eyes excessively, asks frequently to have things repeated).

- handle stressful situations without undue emotional upset (excessive crying, sleeping or eating disturbances, withdrawal, frequent anxiety).

- assume responsibility for personal care (dressing, bathing, feeding self) most of the time.

- show improved motor skills.

DEVELOPMENTAL ALERTS

Check with a health care provider or early childhood specialist if, by the ninth birthday, the child *does not*

- exhibit a good appetite and continued weight gain (some children, especially girls, may already begin to show early signs of an eating disorder).

- experience fewer illnesses.

- show improved motor skills, in terms of agility, speed, and balance.

- understand abstract concepts and use complex thought processes to problem-solve.

- enjoy school and the challenge of learning.

- follow through on multiple-step instructions.

- express ideas clearly and fluently.

- form friendships with other children and enjoy participating in group activities.

11- TO 13-YEAR-OLDS

Children ages 11 to 13

- are less influenced by parents and may exhibit some rebellion.

- place importance on their peer group and allow it to sets standards for behavior.

- worry about what others think.

- choose friends based on common interests.

- gender differences in interests.

- develop awareness and interest in opposite gender.

- begin to question adult authority.

- are often reluctant to attend childcare; are bored or think they can care for themselves.

- may be moody and experience stress over physical changes of puberty.

- may be rebellious as they seek their own identity.

- can think abstractly and apply logic to solving problems.

- have a good command of spoken and written language.

- develop gender characteristics (girls); begin a growth spurt (boys).

- mature early if they have a positive self-image.

- are able to master physical skills necessary for playing games.

Child's Name _____   Age _____
Observer _____   Date _____

DEVELOPMENTAL CHECKLIST

By 10 and 11 Years:	Yes	No	Sometimes
Does the child . . .			
Continue to increase in height and weight?			
Exhibit improving coordination: running, climbing, riding a bike, writing?			

Does the child . . . , continued	Yes	No	Sometimes
Handle stressful situations without becoming overly upset or violent?			
Construct sentences using reasonably correct grammar: nouns, adverbs, verbs, adjectives?			
Understand concepts of time, distance, space, volume?			
Have one or two "best friends"?			
Maintain friendships over time?			
Approach challenges with a reasonable degree of self-confidence?			
Play cooperatively and follow group instructions?			
Begin to show an understanding of moral standards: right from wrong, fairness, honesty, good from bad?			
Look forward to, and enjoy, school?			
Appear to hear well and listen attentively?			
Enjoy reasonably good health, with few episodes of illness or health-related complaints?			
Have a good appetite and enjoy mealtimes?			
Take care of own personal hygiene without assistance?			
Sleep through the night, waking up refreshed and energetic?			

DEVELOPMENTAL ALERTS

Check with a health care provider or early childhood specialist if, by the 11th birthday, the child *does not*

- continue to grow at a rate appropriate for the child's gender.

- show continued improvement of fine motor skills.

- make or keep friends.

- enjoy going to school and show interest in learning (have children's hearing and vision tested; vision and hearing problems affect children's ability to learn and their interest in learning).

- approach new situations with reasonable confidence.

- handle failure and frustration in a constructive manner.

- sleep through the night or experiences prolonged problems with bedwetting, nightmares, or sleepwalking.

Child's Name _____   Age _____
Observer _____   Date _____

DEVELOPMENTAL CHECKLIST

By 12 and 13 Years:	Yes	No	Sometimes
Does the child . . .			
Appear to be growing: increasing height and maintaining a healthy weight (not too thin or too heavy)?			
Understand changes associated with puberty or have an opportunity to learn and ask questions?			
Complain of headaches or blurred vision?			
Have an abnormal posture or curving of the spine?			
Seem energetic and not chronically fatigued?			
Stay focused on a task and complete assignments?			
Remember and carry out complex instructions?			
Sequence, order, and classify objects?			
Use longer and more complex sentence structure?			
Engage in conversation; tell jokes and riddles?			
Enjoy playing organized games and team sports?			
Respond to anger-invoking situations without resorting to violence or physical aggression?			
Begin to understand and solve complex mathematical problems?			
Accept blame for actions on most occasions?			
Enjoy competition?			
Accept and carry out responsibility in a dependable manner?			
Go to bed willingly and wake up refreshed?			
Take pride in appearance; keep self reasonably clean?			

DEVELOPMENTAL ALERTS

Check with a health care provider or early childhood specialist if, by the 13th birthday, the child *does not*

- have movements that are smooth and coordinated.
- have energy sufficient for playing, riding bikes, or engaging in other desired activities.

- stay focused on tasks at hand.

- understand basic cause-and-effect relationships.

- handle criticism and frustration with a reasonable response (physical aggression and excessive crying could be an indication of other, underlying problems).

- exhibit a healthy appetite (frequent skipping of meals is not typical for this age group).

- make and keep friends.

Some content in this section was adapted from Allen, E.A. and Marotz, L., Developmental Profiles: *Pre-birth through Twelve,* (4th ed.), published by Thomson Delmar Learning.

DEVELOPMENTAL MILESTONES BY SKILL

As with the list of milestones by age, this list is not exhaustive, but it can be used to arrange an environment or to plan activities in your room.

BIRTH TO ONE MONTH

Physical	Date Observed
Engages in primarily reflexive motor activity	
Maintains "fetal" position especially when sleeping	
Holds hands in a fist; does not reach for objects	
In prone position, head falls lower than the body's horizontal line with hips flexed and arms and legs hanging down	
Has good upper body muscle tone when supported under the arms	
Cognitive	
Blinks in response to fast-approaching object	
Follows a slowly moving object through a complete 180-degree arc	
Follows objects moved vertically if close to infant's face	
Continues looking about, even in the dark	
Begins to study own hand when lying in tonic neck reflex position	
Prefers to listen to mother's voice rather than a stranger's	
Language	
Cries and fusses as major forms of communication	
Reacts to loud noises by blinking, moving (or stopping), shifting eyes, making a startle response	
Shows preference for certain sounds (music and human voices) by calming down or quieting	
Turns head to locate voices and other sounds	
Makes occasional sounds other than crying	
Social/Emotional	
Experiences a short period of alertness immediately following birth	
Sleeps 17–19 hours a day; is gradually awake and responsive for longer periods	

Social/Emotional, continued	Date Observed
Likes to be held close and cuddled when awake	
Shows qualities of individuality in responding or not responding to similar situations	
Begins to establish emotional attachment or bonding with parents and caregivers	
Begins to develop a sense of security/trust with parents and caregivers; responses to different individuals vary	

ONE TO FOUR MONTHS

Physical	Date Observed
Well developed rooting and sucking reflexes	
In prone position, Landau reflex appears, baby raises head and upper body on arms	
Grasps with entire hand; strength insufficient to hold items	
Movements tend to be large and jerky	
Turns head side to side when in a supine (face up) position	
Begins rolling from front to back by turning head to one side and allowing trunk to follow	
Cognitive	
Fixes on a moving object held at 12 in. (30.5 cm)	
Continues to gaze in direction of moving objects that have disappeared	
Exhibits some sense of size/color/shape recognition of objects in the immediate environment	
Alternates looking at an object, at one or both hands, and then back at the object	
Moves eyes from one object to another	
Focuses on small object and reaches for it; usually follows own hand movements	
Language	
Reacts to sounds (voice, rattle, doorbell); later will search for source by turning head	
Coordinates vocalizing, looking, and body movements in face-to-face exchanges with parent or caregiver	
Babbles or coos when spoken to or smiled at	
Imitates own sounds and vowel sounds produced by others	
Laughs out loud	
Social/Emotional	
Imitates, maintains, terminates, and avoids interactions	
Reacts differently to variations in adult voices	
Enjoys being held and cuddled at times other than feeding and bedtime	

Social/Emotional, continued	Date Observed
Coos, gurgles, and squeals when awake	
Smiles in response to a friendly face or voice	
Entertains self for brief periods by playing with fingers, hands, and toes	

FOUR TO EIGHT MONTHS

Physical	Date Observed
Parachute reflex appears toward end of this stage; swallowing reflex appears	
Uses finger and thumb (pincer grip) to pick up objects	
Reaches for objects with both arms simultaneously; later reaches with one hand	
Transfers objects from one hand to the other; grasps object using palmar grasp	
Handles, shakes, and pounds objects; puts everything in mouth	
Sits alone without support (holds head erect, back straight, arms propped forward for support)	
Cognitive	
Turns toward and locates familiar voices and sounds	
Uses hand, mouth, and eyes in coordination to explore own body, toys, and surroundings	
Imitates actions, such as patty-cake, waving bye-bye, and playing peek-a-boo	
Shows fear of falling from high places, such as changing table, stairs	
Looks over side of crib or high chair for objects dropped; delights in repeatedly throwing objects overboard for adult to retrieve	
Bangs objects together playfully; bangs spoon or toy on table	
Language	
Responds appropriately to own name and simple requests, such as "eat" and "wave bye-bye"	
Imitates some nonspeech sounds, such as cough, tongue click, lip smacking	
Produces a full range of vowels and some consonants: r, s, z, th, and w	
Responds to variations in the tone of voice of others	
Expresses emotions (pleasure, satisfaction, anger) by making different sounds	
Babbles by repeating same syllable in a series: ba, ba, ba	
Social/Emotional	
Delights in observing surroundings; continuously watches people and activities	
Begins to develop an awareness of self as a separate individual from others	
Becomes more outgoing and social in nature: smiles, coos, reaches out	
Distinguishes among, and responds differently, to strangers, teachers, parents, siblings	

Social/Emotional, continued	Date Observed
Responds differently and appropriately to facial expressions: frowns; smiles	
Imitates facial expressions, actions, and sounds	

8 TO 12 MONTHS

Physical	Date Observed
Reaches with one hand leading to grasp an offered object or toy	
Manipulates objects, transferring them from one hand to the other	
Explores new objects by poking with one finger	
Uses deliberate pincer grip to pick up small objects, toys, and finger foods	
Stacks objects; also places objects inside one another	
Releases objects by dropping or throwing; cannot intentionally put an object down	
Begins pulling self to a standing position; begins to stand alone	
Cognitive	
Watches people, objects, and activities in the immediate environment	
Shows awareness of distant objects (15 to 20 feet away) by pointing at them	
Reaches for toys that are visible but out of reach	
Continues to drop first item when other toys or items are offered	
Recognizes the reversal of an object: cup upside down is still a cup	
Imitates activities: hitting two blocks together, playing patty-cake	
Language	
Babbles or jabbers to initiate social interaction; may shout to attract attention	
Shakes head for "no" and may nod for "yes"	
Responds by looking for voice when name is called	
Babbles in sentence-like sequences; followed by jargon (syllables/sounds with language-like inflection)	
Waves "bye-bye"; claps hands when asked	
Says "da-da" and "ma-ma"	
Social/Emotional	
Exhibits a definite fear of strangers; clings to, or hides behind, parent or caregiver ("stranger anxiety"); resists separating from familiar adult ("separation anxiety")	
Enjoys being near, and included in, daily activities of family members and teachers; is becoming more sociable and outgoing	
Enjoys novel experiences and opportunities to examine new objects	

Social/Emotional, continued	Date Observed
Shows need to be picked up and held by extending arms upward, crying, or clinging to adult's legs	
Begins to exhibit assertiveness by resisting caregiver's requests; may kick, scream, or throw self on the floor	

ONE-YEAR-OLDS

Physical	Date Observed
Crawls skillfully and quickly; gets to feet unaided	
Stands alone with feet spread apart, legs stiffened, and arms extended for support	
Walks unassisted near the end of this period (most children); falls often; not always able to maneuver around furniture or toys	
Uses furniture to lower self to floor; collapses backward into a sitting position or falls forward on hands and then sits	
Releases an object voluntarily	
Enjoys pushing or pulling toys while walking	
Cognitive	
Enjoys object-hiding activities: early on, will search same location for a hidden object; later will search in several locations	
Passes toy to other hand when offered a second object ("crossing the midline")	
Manages three to four objects by setting an object aside (on lap or floor) when presented with a new toy	
Puts toys in mouth less often	
Enjoys looking at picture books	
Demonstrates understanding of functional relationships (objects that belong together)	
Language	
Produces considerable "jargon": combines words/sounds into speech-like patterns	
Uses one word to convey an entire thought (holophrastic speech); later, produces two-word phrases to express a complete thought (telegraphic speech)	
Follows simple directions: "Give Daddy the cup"	
Points to familiar persons, animals, and toys when asked	
Identifies three body parts if someone names them: "Show me your nose (toe, ear)"	
Indicates a few desired objects/activities by name: "bye-bye," "cookie"; verbal request is often accompanied by an insistent gesture	
Social/Emotional	
Remains friendly toward others; usually less wary of strangers	
Helps pick up and put away toys	
Plays alone for short periods and does not play cooperatively	

Social/Emotional, continued	Date Observed
Enjoys being held and read to	
Imitates adult actions in play	
Enjoys adult attention; likes to know that an adult is near; gives hugs and kisses	

TWO-YEAR-OLDS

Physical	Date Observed
Walks with a more erect, heel-to-toe pattern; can maneuver around obstacles in pathway	
Runs with greater confidence; has fewer falls	
Squats for long periods while playing	
Climbs stairs unassisted (but not with alternating feet)	
Balances on one foot (for a few moments), jumps up and down, but may fall	
Begins to achieve toilet training (depending on physical and neurological development) although accidents should still be expected; will indicate readiness for toilet training	
Cognitive	
Exhibits better coordinated eye–hand movements; can put objects together, take them apart; fit large pegs into pegboard	
Begins to use objects for purposes other than intended (pushes block around as boat)	
Completes classification based on one dimension (separates toy dinosaurs from toy cars)	
Stares for long moments; seems fascinated by, or engrossed in, figuring out a situation	
Attends to self-selected activities for longer periods of time	
Shows discovery of cause and effect: squeezing the cat makes her scratch	
Language	
Enjoys being read to if allowed to point, make relevant noises, turn pages	
Realizes that language is effective for getting others to respond to needs and preferences	
Uses 50 to 300 different words; vocabulary continuously increasing	
Has broken linguistic code; in other words, much of a two-year-old's talk has meaning to him or her	
Understands more language than can communicate verbally; most two-year-olds' receptive language is more developed than their expressive language	
Utters three- and four-word statements; uses conventional word order to form more complete sentences	

Social/Emotional	Date Observed
Shows empathy and caring	
Continues to use physical aggression if frustrated or angry (more exaggerated in some children); physical aggression lessens as verbal skills improve	
Expresses frustration through temper tantrums; tantrum frequency peaks during this year; cannot be reasoned with while tantrum is in progress	
Finds it difficult to wait or take turns; often impatient	
Enjoys "helping" with household chores; imitates everyday activities	
Orders parents and teachers around; makes demands and expects immediate compliance	

THREE-YEAR-OLDS

Physical	Date Observed
Walks up and down stairs unassisted using alternating feet; may jump from bottom step, landing on both feet	
Balances momentarily on one foot	
Kicks a large ball, catches a large bounced ball with both arms extended	
Feeds self; needs minimal assistance	
Jumps in place	
Pedals a small tricycle or Big Wheel	
Cognitive	
Listens attentively and makes relevant comments during age-appropriate stories, especially those related to home and family events	
Likes to look at books and may pretend to "read" to others or explain pictures	
Enjoys stories with riddles, guessing, and suspense	
Points with fair accuracy to correct pictures when given sound-alike words: keys–cheese; fish–dish; mouse–mouth	
Plays realistically: feeds doll; hooks truck and trailer together	
Places 8 to 10 pegs in pegboard, or 6 round and 6 square blocks in form board	
Language	
Talks about objects, events, and people not present: "Jerry has a pool in his yard"	
Talks about the actions of others: "Daddy's mowing the grass"	
Adds information to what has just been said: "Yeah, and then he grabbed it back"	
Answers simple questions appropriately	
Asks increasing numbers of questions, including location/identity of objects and people	
Uses increased speech forms to keep conversation going: "What did he do next?" "How come she hid?"	

Social/Emotional	Date Observed
Seems to understand taking turns, but not always willing to do so	
Laughs frequently; is friendly and eager to please	
Has occasional nightmares and fears the dark, monsters, or fire	
Joins in simple games and group activities, sometimes hesitantly	
Talks to self often	
Uses objects symbolically in play: block of wood may be a truck, a ramp, a bat	

FOUR-YEAR-OLDS

Physical	Date Observed
Walks a straight line (tape line or chalk line on the floor)	
Hops on one foot	
Pedals and steers a wheeled toy with confidence; avoids obstacles and oncoming "traffic"	
Climbs ladders, trees, playground equipment	
Jumps over objects 5 or 6 in. (12.5 to 15 cm) high; lands with both feet together	
Runs, starts, stops, and moves around obstacles with ease	
Cognitive	
Stacks at least five graduated cubes largest to smallest; builds a pyramid of six blocks	
Indicates if paired words sound the same or different: sheet–feet, ball–wall	
Names 18–20 uppercase letters near the end of this year; may be able to print several and write own name; may recognize some printed words (especially those that have special meaning)	
Some begin to read simple books (alphabet books with few words per page and many pictures)	
Likes stories about how things grow and operate	
Delights in wordplay, creating silly language	
Language	
Uses the prepositions "on," "in," and "under"	
Uses possessives consistently: "hers," "theirs," "baby's"	
Answers "Whose?" "Who?" "Why?" and "How many?"	
Produces elaborate sentence structures	
Uses almost entirely intelligible speech	
Begins to correctly use the past tense of verbs: "Mommy closed the door," "Daddy went to work."	

Social/Emotional	Date Observed
Is outgoing and friendly; overly enthusiastic at times	
Changes moods rapidly and unpredictably; often throws tantrum over minor frustrations; sulk over being left out	
Holds conversations and shares strong emotions with imaginary playmates or companions; invisible friends are common	
Boasts, exaggerates, and "bends" the truth with made-up stories or claims; tests limits with "bathroom" talk	
Cooperates with others; participates in group activities	
Shows pride in accomplishments; seeks frequent adult approval	

FIVE-YEAR-OLDS

Physical	Date Observed
Walks backward, heel to toe	
Walks unassisted up- and down stairs, alternating feet	
Learns to turn somersaults (should be taught the right way to avoid injury)	
Touches toes without flexing knees	
Catches a ball thrown from 3 feet away	
Rides a tricycle or wheeled toy with speed and skillful steering; some learn to ride bicycles, usually with training wheels	
Cognitive	
Forms rectangle from two triangular cuts	
Builds steps with set of small blocks	
Understands concept of same shape, same size	
Sorts objects on the basis of two dimensions, such as color and form	
Sorts objects so that all things in the group have a single common feature	
Understands smallest and shortest; places objects in order from shortest to tallest, smallest to largest	
Language	
Has vocabulary of 1,500 words or more	
Tells a familiar story while looking at pictures in a book	
Uses functional definitions: a ball is to bounce; a bed is to sleep in	
Identifies and names four to eight colors	
Recognizes the humor in simple jokes; makes up jokes and riddles	
Produces sentences with five to seven words; much longer sentences are not unusual	

Social/Emotional	Date Observed
Enjoys friendships; often has one or two special playmates	
Shares toys, takes turns, plays cooperatively (with occasional lapses); is often generous	
Participates in play and activities with other children; suggests imaginative and elaborate play ideas	
Is affectionate and caring, especially toward younger or injured children and animals	
Follows directions and carries out assignments usually; generally does what parent or teacher requests	
Continues to need adult comfort and reassurance, but may be less open in seeking and accepting comfort	

SIX-YEAR-OLDS

Physical	Date Observed
Has increased muscle strength; typically boys are stronger than girls of similar size	
Gains greater control over large and fine motor skills; movements are more precise and deliberate although some clumsiness persists	
Enjoys vigorous physical activity: running, jumping, climbing, and throwing	
Moves constantly, even when trying to sit still	
Has increased dexterity, eye–hand coordination, and improved motor functioning, which facilitate learning to ride a bicycle, swimming, swinging a bat, or kicking a ball	
Enjoys art projects: likes to paint, model with clay, "make things," draw and color, work with wood	
Cognitive	
Shows increased attention; works at tasks for longer periods, although concentrated effort is not always consistent	
Understands simple time markers (today, tomorrow, yesterday) or uncomplicated concepts of motion (cars go faster than bicycles)	
Recognizes seasons and major holidays and the activities associated with each	
Enjoys puzzles, counting and sorting activities, paper-and-pencil mazes, and games that involve matching letters and words with pictures	
Recognizes some words by sight; attempts to sound out words (some may read well by this time)	
Identifies familiar coins: pennies, nickels, dimes, quarters	
Language	
Loves to talk, often nonstop; may be described as a chatterbox	
Carries on adult-like conversations; asks many questions	
Learns 5 to 10 new words daily; vocabulary consists of 10,000 to 14,000 words	

Language, continued	Date Observed
Uses appropriate verb tenses, word order, and sentence structure	
Uses language (not tantrums or physical aggression) to express displeasure: "That's mine! Give it back, you dummy."	
Talks self through steps required in simple problem-solving situations (although the "logic" may be unclear to adults)	
Social/Emotional	
Experiences mood swings: "best friends" then "worst enemies;" loving then uncooperative and irritable; especially unpredictable toward mother or primary caregiver	
Becomes less dependent on parents as friendship circle expands; still needs closeness and nurturing but has urges to break away and "grow up"	
Needs and seeks adult approval, reassurance, and praise; may complain excessively about minor hurts to gain more attention	
Continues to be egocentric; still sees events almost entirely from own perspective: views everything and everyone as there for child's own benefit	
Easily disappointed and frustrated by self-perceived failure	
Has difficulty composing and soothing self; cannot tolerate being corrected or losing at games; may sulk, cry, refuse to play, or reinvent rules to suit own purposes	

SEVEN-YEAR-OLDS

Physical	Date Observed
Exhibits large and fine motor control that is more finely tuned	
Tends to be cautious in undertaking more challenging physical activities, such as climbing up or jumping down from high places	
Practices a new motor skill repeatedly until mastered, and then moves on to something else	
Finds floor more comfortable than furniture when reading or watching television; legs often in constant motion	
Uses knife and fork appropriately, but inconsistently	
Tightly grasps pencil near the tip; rests head on forearm, lowers head almost to the table top when doing pencil-and-paper tasks	
Cognitive	
Understands concepts of space and time in both logical and practical ways: a year is "a long time"; 100 miles is "far away"	
Begins to grasp Piaget's concepts of conservation (the shape of a container does not necessarily reflect what it can hold)	
Gains a better understanding of cause and effect: "If I'm late for school again, I'll be in big trouble."	

Cognitive, continued	Date Observed
Tells time by the clock and understands calendar time—days, months, years, seasons	
Plans ahead: "I'm saving this cookie for tonight."	
Shows marked fascination with magic tricks; enjoys putting on "shows" for parents and friends	

Language	
Enjoys storytelling; likes to write short stories, tell imaginative tales	
Uses adult-like sentence structure and language in conversation; patterns reflect cultural and geographical differences	
Becomes more precise and elaborate in use of language; greater use of descriptive adjectives and adverbs	
Uses gestures to illustrate conversations	
Criticizes own performance: "I didn't draw that right," "Her picture is better than mine."	
Verbal exaggeration commonplace: "I ate 10 hot dogs at the picnic."	

Social/Emotional	
Is cooperative and affectionate toward adults and less frequently annoyed with them; sees humor in everyday happenings	
Likes to be the "teacher's helper"; eager for teacher's attention and approval but less obvious about seeking it	
Seeks out friendships; friends are important, but can stay busy if no one is available	
Quarrels less often, although squabbles and tattling continue in both one-on-one and group play	
Complains that family decisions are unjust, that a particular sibling gets to do more or is given more	
Blames others for own mistakes; makes up alibis for personal shortcomings: "I could have made a better one, but my teacher didn't give me enough time."	

EIGHT-YEAR-OLDS

Physical	Date Observed
Enjoys vigorous activity; likes to dance, roller blade, swim, wrestle, bicycle, fly kites	
Seeks opportunities to participate in team activities and games: soccer, baseball, kickball	
Exhibits significant improvement in agility, balance, speed, and strength	
Copies words and numbers from blackboard with increasing speed and accuracy; has good eye–hand coordination	
Possesses seemingly endless energy	

Cognitive	Date Observed
Collects objects; organizes and displays items according to more complex systems; bargains and trades with friends to obtain additional pieces	
Saves money for small purchases; eagerly develops plans to earn cash for odd jobs; studies catalogues and magazines for items to purchase	
Begins taking an interest in what others think and do; understands there are differences of opinion, cultures, distant countries	
Accepts challenge and responsibility with enthusiasm; delights in being asked to perform tasks at home and in school; interested in being rewarded	
Likes to read and work independently; spends considerable time planning and making lists	
Understands perspective (shadow, distance, shape); drawings reflect more realistic portrayal of objects	
Language	
Delights in telling jokes and riddles	
Understands and carries out multiple-step instructions (up to five steps); may need directions repeated because of not listening to the entire request	
Enjoys writing letters or sending e-mail messages to friends; includes imaginative and detailed descriptions	
Uses language to criticize and compliment others; repeats slang and curse words	
Understands and follows rules of grammar in conversation and written form	
Is intrigued with learning secret word codes and using code language	
Converses fluently with adults; can think and talk about past and future: "What time are we leaving to get to the swim meet next week?"	
Social/Emotional	
Begins forming opinions about moral values and attitudes; declares things right or wrong	
Plays with two or three "best" friends, most often the same age and gender; also enjoys spending some time alone	
Seems less critical of own performance but is easily frustrated when unable to complete a task or when the product does not meet expectations	
Enjoys team games and activities; values group membership and acceptance by peers	
Continues to blame others or makes up alibis to explain own shortcomings or mistakes	
Enjoys talking on the telephone with friends	

Some content in this section adapted from Allen, E.A. and Marotz, L., *Developmental Profiles: Pre-birth through Twelve* (4th ed.), published by Thomson Delmar Learning.

PLAY MATERIALS FOR CHILDREN

Children construct their own understanding of the world around them as they interact with appropriate materials and with other people. Teachers play an important role in providing choices of good quality playthings that match children's developmental abilities and interests. When budgets are limited, it is vital for teachers to select toys and materials that will provide optimum learning opportunities. Creative teachers learn how to "scrounge" for toys and to make playthings out of recycled materials.

CRITERIA FOR SELECTING PLAY EQUIPMENT FOR YOUNG CHILDREN

A young child's playthings should be as free of detail as possible.

- Too much detail hampers a child's freedom to express himself.

- "Unstructured" toys, which allow the imagination free rein, include blocks, construction sets, clay, sand, and paints.

A good plaything should stimulate children to do things for themselves.

- Equipment that makes the child a spectator may entertain but has little or no play value.

- Play equipment should encourage children to explore and create or offer dramatic play potential.

Young children need large, easily manipulated playthings.

- Toys too small can be frustrating because the child's undeveloped muscular coordination cannot handle smaller forms and shapes.

- A child's muscles develop through play, so equipment should allow for climbing and balancing.

The material of which a plaything is constructed has an important role in the play of the young child.

- Warmth and pleasurable touch are significant (wood and cloth have been established as the most satisfactory materials).

- The plaything's durability is of utmost importance.

- Play materials must be sturdy; axles and wheels must be able to support a child's weight.

- Children hate to see their toys break.

- Some materials break readily, proving them to be expensive.

The toy must "work."

- Be sure parts move correctly.

- Toys should be easy to maintain.

A plaything's construction should be simple enough for a child to comprehend.

- This strengthens children's understanding and experience of the world around them.

- Mechanics should be visible and easily grasped; small children will take them apart to see how they tick.

A plaything should encourage cooperative play.

- Provide an environment that stimulates children to work and play together.

The total usefulness of the plaything must be considered when comparing prices.

- Will it last several children through several stages of their playing lives?

The lists in the following sections suggest the materials that are priorities for children at particular levels of development.

FOR YOUNG INFANTS (BIRTH THROUGH SIX MONTHS)

- unbreakable mirrors that can be attached low on walls, or near changing tables and cribs
- washable stuffed toys or rag dolls with stitched faces and eyes
- mobiles and visuals hung out of reach
- grasping toys: simple rattles, squeeze toys, keys on ring, clutch or texture balls
- hanging toys for batting
- wrist or ankle bells

FOR OLDER, MOBILE INFANTS (7 THROUGH 12 MONTHS)

- soft rubber animals for grasping
- simple one-piece vehicles 6-8 in., with large wheels
- grasping toys for skill development: toys on suction cups, stacking rings, nesting cups, squeeze toys, plastic pop beads, bean bags, busy boxes
- containers and objects to fill and dump
- small cloth-, plastic-, and board books
- soft cloth or foam blocks for stacking
- simple floating objects for water play
- balls of all kinds, including some with special effects
- low soft climbing platforms
- large unbreakable mirrors
- infant swings for outdoors
- recorded music and songs

FOR TODDLERS (ONE TO THREE YEARS)

For Fine Motor Skills

- nesting materials
- sand and water play toys: funnels, colanders, small sand tools

- simple activity boxes with doors, lids, switches; more complex after about 18 months: turning knob or key

- pegboards with large pegs

- 4- to 5-piece stacking materials

- pop beads and stringing beads

- simple 3- to 5-piece puzzles, with knobs, familiar shapes

- simple matching materials

- books, including tactile books, cloth books, plastic books, and board picture books

For Gross Motor Skills

- push and pull toys

- simple doll carriages and wagons

- stable riding toys with four wheels and no pedals

- balls of all sizes

- tunnels for crawling through

- tumbling mats and low climbing platforms

For Pretend Play

- small wood or plastic people and animal figures

- small cars and trucks

- dolls

- plastic dishes and pots and pans

- doll beds

- hats

- simple dress-ups

- telephones

- scarves and fabrics

For Sensory Play

- recorded music and player

- play dough

- fingerpaint

- large nontoxic crayons

- sturdy paper

- simple musical instruments

FOR CHILDREN AGES THREE THROUGH FIVE

For Gross Motor Play

- small wagons and wheelbarrows

- replicas of adult tools for pushing and pretend play, such as lawn mower, shopping cart

- scooters

- tricycles and other vehicles with steering ability

- riding toys for more than one child

- balls of all sizes, especially 10- to 12-in. balls for kicking and throwing

- hollow plastic bat and lightweight ball

- jump rope

- stationary outdoor climbing equipment

- slides and ladders

- outdoor building materials, tires, and other loose parts

Exploration and Mastery Play Materials

- sand and water play: measures, funnels, tubes, sand tools

- construction materials: unit blocks, large hollow blocks

- Lego-type plastic interlocking blocks

- puzzles, including fit-in puzzles and large, simple jigsaw puzzles with varying numbers of pieces, according to children's age

- pattern-making materials: beads for stringing, pegboards, mosaic boards, feltboards, color cubes

- dressing, lacing, and stringing: sewing cards and dressing frames

- collections of small plastic objects for matching, sorting, and ordering by color, shape, size, or other category concepts

- simple, concrete number materials for counting and matching to numerals

- measuring materials: scales, measuring cups for liquids

- science materials: magnifying glass, color paddles, objects from the natural world, including pets

- beginning computer programs

- games: dominoes; lotto games; bingo by color, number, or picture; first board games that use concepts such as color or counting; Memory

- books of all kinds: picture books, realistic story books, alphabet picture books, poetry books, information books

- writing center materials: clipboards, colored pencils, old calendars, envelopes, notepads, stationary, rubber stamps and ink pads, rulers, magnetic letters, stencil shapes, stickers, file cards, and office materials

For Pretend Play

- dolls of various ethnic and gender appearance, with clothes and other accessories and furniture

- housekeeping equipment

- variety of dress-ups, including those related to various roles and themes

- transportation toys

- hand puppets

- animal and human figures for play scenes

- full length, unbreakable mirror

For Creative Play

- art and craft materials: crayons, markers, easel, paint-brushes, paint and fingerpaint, varieties of paper, chalk-board and chalk, safety scissors, glue, collage materials, clay and play dough, and tools to use with them

- workbench with hammer, saw, and nails

- musical instruments

- recorded music for singing, movement and dancing, listening, and for using with rhythm instruments

FOR CHILDREN AGES SIX THROUGH EIGHT

For Gross Motor Play

- balls and sports equipment for beginning team play, such as soccer, baseball

- complex climbing structures: ropes, ladders, rings, hanging bars

- materials for target practice

- mats for acrobatics

- bicycles and scooters

For Exploration and Mastery Play

- construction materials for large constructions and for creating models, including metal parts and nuts and bolts

- puzzles: 100-piece jigsaw puzzles, three-dimensional puzzles, such as Rubik's cubes

- craft materials for braiding, weaving, knitting, leather crafting, jewelry making, sewing

- pattern-making materials: mosaic tiles, geometric puzzles

- games: word games, simple card games, reading and spelling games, number and counting games, beginning strategy games such as checkers

- materials for specific learning: printing materials, math manipulatives, measuring materials, science materials, and computer programs for language arts, number and concept development, and problem-solving activities

- books at a variety of levels for beginning readers—see the Resources list in the supplement

For Creative Activities

- variety of markers, colored pencils, chalks, paintbrushes and paints, art papers for tracing and drawing

- clay and tools, including pottery wheel

- workbench with wood and variety of tools

- real instruments such as guitars and recorders

- music for singing and movement

- audiovisual materials for independent use

Some ideas adapted from *The Right Stuff for Children Birth to 8: Selecting play materials to support development.* M. Bronson. Washington, DC: NAEYC, 1995.

UNCONVENTIONAL MATERIALS

Remember that recycled materials and other loose parts have many uses for exploration and creativity. These materials can be valuable tools in a number of curriculum areas:

- empty plastic containers, such as detergent bottles, bleach bottles, old refrigerator containers, which can be used for constructing scoops, storing art materials, and so on

- buttons—all colors and sizes—which are excellent for collages and assemblages, as well as sorting, counting, matching, and so on

- egg shells, which can be washed, dried, and colored with food coloring for art projects

- coffee or shortening cans and lids, which can be covered with adhesive paper and used for storage of art supplies, games, and manipulatives materials

- magazines with colorful pictures, which are excellent for making collages, murals, and posters

- scraps of fabric, such as felt, silk, cotton, oil cloth, and so on, which can be used to make "fabric boards" with the name of each fabric written under a small swatch attached to the board, as well as for collages, puppets, and so on

- yarn scraps, which can be used for separating buttons into sets; also for art activities

- styrofoam scraps

- scraps of lace, rick rack, or decorative trim

- bottles with sprinkler tops, which are excellent for water play and for mixing water as children fingerpaint

- wallpaper books of discontinued patterns

- paper doilies

- discarded wrapping paper

- paint color cards from paint/hardware stores

- old paintbrushes

- old jewelry and beads

- old muffin tins, which are effective for sorting small objects and mixing paint

- tongue depressors or ice cream sticks, which can be used as counters for math and are good for art construction projects, stick puppets, and so on

- wooden clothespins, which can be used for making "people," for construction projects, for hanging up paintings to dry

Adapted from Mayesky, M., *Creative Activities for Young Children* (7th ed.), published by Thomson Delmar Learning.

BASIC PROGRAM EQUIPMENT AND MATERIALS FOR AN EARLY CHILDHOOD CENTER

If you are responsible for ordering supplies for your classroom or early childhood program, the following guidelines will be useful.

INDOOR EQUIPMENT

The early childhood room should be arranged into well-planned areas of interest—such as the housekeeping and doll corner, block building area, and so on—to encourage children to play in small groups throughout the playroom, engaging in activities of their special interest, rather than attempting to play in one large group.

The early childhood center must provide selections of indoor play equipment from many areas of interest. Selection should be of sufficient quantities so that children can participate in a wide range of activities. Many pieces of equipment can be homemade. Consider the age and developmental levels of the children when making selections.

Playroom Furnishings

- *Tables:* Seat four to six children (18 in. high for three-year-olds, 20–22 in. high for four- and five-year-olds).

- *Chairs:* 10 in. high for three-year-olds, 12–14 in. high for four- and five-year-olds.

- *Open shelves:* 26 in. high, 12 in. deep, 12 in. between shelves.

- *Lockers:* 12 in. wide, 12 in. deep, 32–36 in. high.

Housekeeping or Doll Corner

Item	Number Recommended for 10 Children
Dolls	3
Doll clothes	Variety
Doll bed—should be large enough for a child to get into, bedding	1
Doll high chair	1
Small table, four chairs	1 set
Tea party dishes	6-piece set with tray
Stove—child size, approximately 24 in. high, 23 in. long, 12 in. wide	1
Sink—child size, approximately 24 in. high, 23 in. long, 12 in. wide	1
Refrigerator—child size, approximately 28 in. high, 23" in. long, 12 in. wide	1
Pots and pans, empty food cartons, measuring cups, spoons, and so on	Variety
Mop, broom, dustpan	1
Ironing board and iron	1
Clothespins and clothesline	1
Toy telephones	2
Dress-up box—men's and women's hats, neckties, pocketbooks, shoes, old dresses, scarves, jewelry, and so on	Variety
Mirror	1

Art Supplies

Item	Number Recommended for 10 Children
Newsprint paper 18 × 24 in.	1 ream
Colored paper—variety	3 packages
Large crayons	10 boxes
Tempera paint—red, yellow, blue, black, white	1 can each
Long-handled paintbrushes—making a stroke from 1/2 in. to 1 in. wide	10–12
Easels	1
Fingerpaint paper—glazed paper such as shelf, freezer, or butcher's paper	1 roll
Paste	1 quart
Blunt scissors	10
Collage—collection of bits of colored paper, cut-up gift wrappings, ribbons, cotton, string, scraps of fabric, and so on, for pasting	Variety
Magazines for cutting and pasting	Variety

Item	Number Recommended for 10 Children
Clay—play dough, homemade dough clay	50 pounds
Cookie cutters, rolling pins	Variety
Smocks or aprons to protect children's clothes	10

Block Building Area

Item	Number Recommended for 10 Children
Unit blocks—purchased or homemade (directions are available)	276 pieces, 11 shapes
Large, lightweight blocks	Variety
Small wooden or rubber animals and people	Variety
Small trucks, airplanes, cars, and boats	12
Medium airplanes	3
Medium boats	2
Medium-sized trucks—12 in. to 24 in.	3

Music Corner

- record player, tape player, CD player
- suitable records, tapes, and CDs
- rhythm instruments
- dress-up scarves for dancing

Manipulative Toys

Item	Number Recommended for 10 Children
Wooden inlay puzzles—approximately 5 to 20 pieces	6
Color cone	1
Nested blocks	1
Pegboards—variety of shapes and sizes	1
Large spools and beads for stringing	2 sets
Toys that have parts that fit into one another	2
Lotto games	2
Dominoes	1

Books and Stories

A carefully selected book collection (20 to 30 books) for the various age levels should include the following:

- transportation, birds and animals, family life
- community helpers, science, nonsense rhymes
- Mother Goose rhymes, poems, and stories
- homemade picture books
- collection of pictures classified by subject
- library books to enrich the collection

Nature Study and Science

- aquarium or fish bowls
- plastic materials
- magnifying glass, prism, magnet, thermometers
- growing indoor plants, garden plot
- additional material such as stones, leaves, acorns, birds' nests, caterpillars, worms, tadpoles, and so on

Woodworking Center

Basic woodworking operations are

- sanding.
- gluing.
- hammering.
- holding (with a vise or clamp).
- fastening (with screws).
- drilling.
- sawing.

Materials for a woodworking center include

- a sturdy workbench (or table).
- woodworking tools, such as broad-headed nails 3/4 to 1-1/2 in. long, C-clamp or vise (to hold wood), flat-headed hammer weighing about 12 ounces for beginning

woodworking experiences (later a claw hammer may be added), and a 14 in. saw with 10 teeth to the inch.

■ soft white pine lumber scraps (it is difficult to drive nails into hardwood; plywood is not suitable either); packing boxes of soft pine can be disassembled and used for hammering work.

Sand Play

■ For outdoors, sand should be confined so it is not scattered over the rest of the playground.

■ Outdoor area should be large enough for several children to move about without crowding each other.

■ A 10 to 12 in. ledge around a sandbox can serve as a boundary and provide children with a working surface or a seat.

■ Keep sand 6 to 8 in. below the top of the ledge so that it is less likely to spill out.

■ Sand should be about 18 in. deep so children can dig or make tunnels.

■ Provide drainage on the bottom of the sandbox by using 4 to 5 in. of gravel.

■ Provide this basic equipment: plastic or metal kitchen utensils—cups, spoons, pails, shovels, sifters, funnels, scoops, and bowls.

Water Play

■ This can be either an indoor or outdoor activity, depending on the climate.

■ Use clear plastic water basins on a stand with wheels to allow them to be moved to any area of a room.

■ When using plastic basins, children can see through the sides and the bottom.

■ For tables on a carpeted floor, use a plastic runner to protect the carpet.

■ Provide these materials: clear tubing, sponges, strainers, funnels, corks, pitchers, and measuring cups; for added interest, include rotary beaters, spoons, small bowls, plastic basters, and straws.

OUTDOOR EQUIPMENT

Outdoor play equipment should be grouped according to use. For example, plan for both active and quiet play; allow for free areas for use of wheel toys. Suggested basic outdoor play equipment for the early childhood program includes

- climbing structure(s)
- large and small packing boxes
- slides
- swings with canvas seats
- wagons and wheelbarrows
- pedal toys—tricycles, cars, and so on
- sandbox with spoons, shovels, pails, and so on
- balls
- a variety of salvage materials: rubber tires, tire tubes, lengths of garden hose, ropes, and cardboard boxes

Note: Many activities, such as housekeeping play and art activities, at times can be transferred to the outdoor area.

Use this checklist to evaluate your playground setup:

- ☐ Pathways are clear and spacious enough between areas so that traffic flows well and equipment does not obstruct the children's movement.
- ☐ Space and equipment are organized so that children are readily visible and easily supervised by adults.
- ☐ Different activity areas are separated. (Tricycle paths are separate from swings; sand box is separate from climbing area.)
- ☐ Open space is available for active play.
- ☐ There is some space for quiet play.
- ☐ Dramatic play can be set up outdoors, as space is available.
- ☐ Art activities can be set up outdoors.
- ☐ A portion of the play area is covered for use in wet weather.
- ☐ A storage area is available for play equipment.
- ☐ A drinking fountain is available.
- ☐ The area has readily accessible restrooms.

OBSERVATION AND ASSESSMENT

A variety of tools can be used to assess children's development. Using assessment tools in conjunction with developmental milestones helps caregivers recognize a child's developmental accomplishments as well as determine the child's next growth steps. Not all children will be developing at the same rate, in the same way. The teacher needs to observe each child to determine the level to which each child is performing independently so that instruction can begin. This knowledge is useful in planning curriculum, designing the room environment for success, and in establishing appropriate guidance techniques that help children manage their own behavior. No doubt your college practicum experience taught you the logistics of observing: using objective description and recording specific, dated, brief, and factual information. Observation can take many forms; the most common include the following:

- anecdotal records

- running records

- checklists

- time or event sampling

Anecdotal records are brief notes kept by the teacher while the child is performing a task. At first this may seem daunting, but it will become part of your everyday routine. Keep a small spiral notebook and pen or pencil in your pocket. When a child begins an activity, watch what the child does and write down three or four things that you actually observe the child doing. Remember to note the facts and only the facts. For example:

Roberto in blocks, setting long ones aside and forming shapes with small blocks.

Eyes focused on work, no response when David and Jacob came in.

Jacob took long block, Roberto asked for it back. Did not react when Jacob did not, but removed all other long blocks.

As time permits, probably during naptime, the brief notes are turned into a full scenario so that anyone could read the record at a later date:

ANECDOTAL RECORD

Child's Name: Roberto M.   Age: 4 yr. 5 mo.
Observer's Name: Jorge   Date: May 25, 2005

What actually happened/What I saw	Developmental Interpretation (Select 1 or 2 of the following)	
Setting: Block area	Interest in learning	
Roberto entered the block area and began to remove blocks from the shelves immediately. He set all the long blocks to the side and began to create shapes with the small unit blocks. He kept his eyes on his work, making no response when David and Jacob came in and began to build together, talking to Roberto as they built. After a few minutes, Jacob grabbed one of the long blocks. Roberto said, "You have to give that back. I need it for my zoo." Jacob did not return the block, and Roberto said nothing more but moved all the other long blocks far from where Jacob was.	Self esteem/self concept	
	Cultural acceptance	
	Problem-solving	
	Interest in real-life mathematical concepts	X
	Interactions with adults	
	Literacy	
	Interactions with peers	
	Language expression/comprehension	
	Self regulation	X
	Safe/healthy behavior	
	Self-help skills	
	Gross motor skills	
	Fine motor skills	X

ANECDOTAL RECORD

Child's Name: _____   Date: _____

Observer's Name: _____

What actually happened/What I saw	Developmental Interpretation (Select 1 or 2 of the following)	
	Interest in learning	
	Self esteem/self concept	
	Cultural acceptance	
	Problem solving	
	Interest in real-life mathematical concepts	
	Interactions with adults	
	Literacy	
	Interactions with peers	
	Language expression/comprehension	
	Self regulation	
	Safe/healthy behavior	
	Self-help skills	
	Gross motor skills	
	Fine motor skills	

RUNNING RECORD

Another form of authentic assessment is the running record, which covers a longer span of time and gives significantly more information than an anecdotal record. Often it may have a specific developmental focus such as "social interactions." A running record gives you information about other developmental areas because of its very detailed nature. This form of observation requires the caregiver to not be involved with children for several minutes while writing the observation. You will be setting yourself apart from the children and writing continuously, in as much detail as possible. You will write what the child does and says, by herself and in interactions with other people and materials. Use phrases that are objective as previously described. Avoid interpretative and judgmental language. Note that the format for this form of assessment is two columns. The left column is for writing the actual observations and the right column is for connecting the observations to aspects of development. Remember to date all observations so you can notice developmental change over time.

RUNNING RECORD

Child's Name: Trish H.   Age: 5 yr. 5 mo.
Observer's Name: Jorge   Date: April 27, 2005
Developmental Focus: Social interactions with peers

■ Trish is working in the writing center, writing in her journal. Cassie sits down beside her and begins to write in her journal also. Trish looks up from her work and smiles at Cassie. Cassie says she wants to make a card for her sister who is sick. Trish looks at Cassie with a frown on her face and asks "Is she in the hospital?" Cassis says she is, and asks Trish to help her write the words "Get better soon, I miss you." Trish puts her journal aside and helps Cassie. When Cassie grabs the red marker, Trish says, "I need that back so I can draw a heart here for you. The girls finish the card.	Participates in cooperative activities	
	Early literacy/expressive language	
	Expresses empathy	
	Communicates knowledge of growing skills	
	Self regulation/controls emotions	
■ They then go to join Seth and Sam who are throwing bean bags into a target in the corner. Trish says she wants to be the one who counts the number of successful throws this time, as Sam did it last time. She counts 6 for Seth, 3 for Sam, and 4 for Cassie. Then she says "My turn." She throws the bean bag overhand, using her right hand, and is accurate 4 times out of 5. She says to Cassie, "I can throw better now that my Dad showed me how to aim."	Stands up for own rights	
	Asks for what she needs	
	Gross motor skills	
	Math skill	
	Self awareness	

CHECKLIST

A checklist is often used as a means of assessment because it is one of the easiest assessment tools to use. A checklist consists of a predetermined list of developmental criteria for which the observer indicates "yes" or "no." The observer reads the developmental criteria and makes a checkmark if the decision is a "yes." The criteria should be clearly observable. This form of assessment requires that additional notes be recorded. Many teachers design their own checklists to fit the specific needs of their program. The following checklist is an example of one that might be used to assess social skills of children.

SOCIAL SKILLS CHECKLIST

Child's Name: Age: yr.   mo.
Observer's Name:

Skills	Dates
■ Desires to/can work near other children	
■ Interacts with other children	
■ Takes turns with other children	
■ Enters play with others in positive manner	
■ Shares materials and supplies	
■ Stands up for own rights in positive manner	
■ Forms friendships with peers	
■ Engages in positive commentary on other children's work	
■ Shows empathy	
■ Negotiates compromises with other children	
■ Demonstrates prosocial behavior	
■ Participates in cooperative group activities	
■ Resolves conflicts with adult prompts	
■ Resolves conflicts without adult prompts	

Make checklists for each center in your classroom and hang them on clipboards. When you observe the children at play in each center, check off skills by placing a date in the appropriate box.

The last type of observation that a teacher should perform is a time or event sampling. These are similar in focus, but different, too. A *time sampling* asks the teacher to set a timer, and each time the timer goes off, the teacher looks at a particular child and writes down what the child is doing. Again, only the facts are written, nothing else. For example:

> *The timer is set to go off every 10 minutes. I will look at Johnny and see what he is doing when I hear the timer. The timer goes off, I look at Johnny. Johnny is wandering with no apparent focus, looking around to see what everyone else is doing. Maria invites him to play at the water table with her. Johnny goes and begins pouring water from one cup to another. The timer goes off again, Johnny is watching Jacob and David building with blocks. He is sitting, not speaking or doing anything but watching.*

As mentioned, an *event sampling* is similar to a time sampling, only the teacher looks at events instead of being directed by a timer. The teacher zeros in on an event and writes down all things that she sees pertaining to the event. For example:

> *Observation of the play dough activity*
>
> *Trish, Cassie, and Sam come first to the play dough table. Sam begins to roll his play dough flat, using a rolling pin. Trish and Cassie are manipulating the dough and talking with each other about Cassie's birthday party last week. Sam reaches over and takes a lump of Cassie's play dough. She says, "Sam!" and looks at Trish, saying to her "He always does that." Sam does not react to the comment, but begins to form small circles of play dough. He reaches one over to Cassie and says, "Here, I made you a chocolate chip cookie." Cassie asks, "For my birthday?" Sam nods and smiles.*
>
> *Next children to come to play dough are Roberto and David. They begin to form small lumps and add wheels, making car sounds as they move them around the table. They stay at the table for 15 minutes.*

Assessment and observation may seem overwhelming as you begin your career in early childhood. Do not shy away from it. Take the challenge and begin to look for the positive aspects of learning and mastering a new skill. Picture yourself as a student in your classroom and imagine what it is like to perfect something your teacher has just asked you to do. How does it make you feel? Now begin.

CURRICULUM AND LESSON PLANS

Teachers, no matter whether they work with babies, preschoolers, or school-aged children, are involved in a cycle of planning to create developmentally appropriate learning experiences. That cycle begins and ends with observation, and observation occurs as well throughout the cycle. In addition, teachers use their observations to assess children's development in relation to specific goals set by the program or school. They also use their knowledge of individual children's interests and experiences to create meaningful learning experiences that will support progress toward those goals. The cycle continues as teachers continue to observe to see how well their plans have succeeded and if there are needed modifications. Planning curriculum is purposeful and specific to the particular group and individuals within the group.

In addition to this cycle of careful planning, however, teachers also have to be prepared for the unexpected. You have the day planned for outdoor activities and there is an unexpected rainstorm. What will you do? It is your day off and you get a call at the last minute to cover for a coworker who is ill. You find out that nothing has been planned. What activities can you implement quickly? You were promised that the materials you needed for your planned art activity would be on site when you arrived at work, but there was a shipping delay and they aren't there. What is an alternative activity you can easily set up and implement? Being prepared at all times with a few backup activities will make your job much less stressful. Some of the activities listed here require only a few materials. You might want to be sure that these be on hands at all times. When teachers have supplies of open-ended materials, children can find endless possibilities that match their developmental level.

- tapes or CDs for creative movement indoors, with scarves and streamers for props

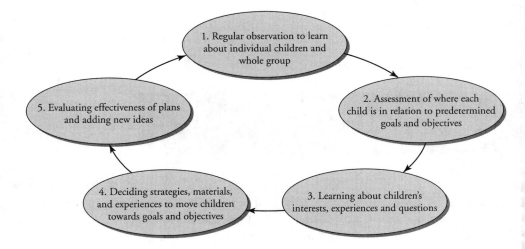

- rhythm instruments to play along with the tapes to have a parade

- an obstacle course, created by moving furniture, and allowing children to maneuver under tables, around shelves, over chairs, and so on

- a collection of Nerf balls and a target or container, to allow children to practice throwing skills indoors

- water, dishpans or water table, and appropriate utensils for sensory exploration

- scraps of fabric, paper scraps, and other recycled materials for gluing on collage

- boxes, paper towel rolls, glue, and paint for box construction

- flour, salt, and other materials for making an easy play dough recipe with children's assistance

- large sheets of butcher paper for children to make life-size self-portraits, tracing around one another with markers, filling in their clothing and hair, and then posting up to measure height

- puzzles and other manipulatives that have been stored elsewhere and are not part of the materials used every day

- a collection of containers and lids of various sizes for matching

- a collection of buttons of various shapes and colors, and muffin tins for sorting, classifying, and doing math games

- large cardboard cartons saved in the closet for use as houses, vehicles, or tunnels; children can paint them to suit the purpose

- the ingredients and a recipe for making individual muffins for snack

- a book of silly poems that you have been saving for a treat

- an activity for the children to make up a story with everyone adding an idea or sentence; write the story on chart paper for a literacy experience and post it for parents to enjoy.

- an impromptu performance where children can sing a song, recite a nursery rhyme, or tell a story of their choice; this can be recorded on video or tape recorder for later enjoyment and sharing with families

- a guessing game, based on children's developmental level (for youngest children, it could be guessing an animal based on sound or other clues; for older children, it could be rhyming words, words that start with a certain letter, and so on)

Use your imagination and remember what children's favorite past activities have been. A number of Web sites offer sample lesson plans for teachers. When downloading lesson plans from the Internet or another source, be sure each plan includes

- objective or goal of the lesson.

- materials needed.

- directions for the activity.

- appropriate age group information.

- developmental appropriateness.

Check the resources section of this manual for a list of Web sites with lesson plans and other free materials for teachers. Remember that the best curriculum is that created by a teacher's knowledge of what individual children can do, need to work on, and are interested in. Even when using plans that originate elsewhere, teacher adaptations will make them appropriate for individual situations.

BOOKS FOR CHILDREN

Reading aloud is a wonderful gift that you can give to children. Through sharing an interesting book, you introduce them to a world they might not otherwise be able to visit. You can travel anywhere you like; you can have experiences that are outside the realm of your current environment; you can participate in wonderful fantasies; you can be saddened and then uplifted.

Children's desire to read and the ability to do so is fostered through being read to from the time they are born. Even babies can enjoy looking at picture books and hearing simple stories. Preschoolers love to have favorite books read to them over and over again. As children move into the school years, they can sustain their interest in books that are long and are divided into chapters. When they realize the joy that comes from good books, they are more motivated to read on their own.

Many textbooks provide suggestions for setting up reading corners and providing books for children to read by themselves. This section will focus on books that you can read aloud to children in small or large groups. Remember that the more you read, the better you will become at doing so. When the books have been enjoyed in a group setting, add them to the book corner for children to read alone. In addition, teachers often create lending arrangements, where children can take home books for their parents to read and then return. Teachers who believe in the importance of reading choose the best of children's literature and involve families in reading.

HOW TO GET CHILDREN TO LISTEN AND WANT MORE

- Read to children regularly, individually and in groups. Schedule a time each day for reading. This might be toward the end of the day when children are tired and will enjoy the inactivity. Make sure the setting is comfortable.

- Choose books that you also enjoy, perhaps one you read as a child, or those you find on lists of good books for children. Preview the book before presenting it to the children. You may find passages that you will want to shorten.

- The first time you read a book, state the title and author. Research some interesting facts about the author and share them with the children. If there is an illustrator, include that information as well.

- If you are reading to a large group, position yourself so that you are slightly higher than the children are. In this way, your voice will project more easily.

- If you are reading to a small group, sit among them in a more intimate placement. This will draw them to you and the book.

- Occasionally stop and ask, "What do you think is going to happen next?"

- Read at a pace that will allow children to build mental images of the characters or setting. Change your pace to coincide with the action of the story. Slow your pace and lower you voice during a suspenseful spot. Speed it up a little when the action is moving quickly.

- Allow time for discussion only if children want to do so. Let them voice fears, ask questions, or share their thoughts about the book. Do not turn it into a quiz or need to interpret the story.

- Practice reading aloud, trying to vary your expression or your tone of voice.

- If you are reading a chapter book to older children, create a display containing images or information pertaining to the book you are reading. A map will allow children to pinpoint places mentioned in the story. Pictures, charts, or time lines will also add to the display. Objects or foods mentioned in the book add another dimension.

- Again, with chapter books for older children, find a stopping place each day that will create some suspense. You want the children to be eager to get back to the book the next day.

- When you pick up the book the next day, ask if they remember what had happened just before you stopped reading.

WHAT NOT TO DO

- Don't read a book that you do not enjoy; your feelings will be sensed by the children.

- Don't continue reading a book when it becomes obvious that it was a poor choice. If you preview the book before presenting it to the children, you may avoid this kind of mistake.

- Don't always choose a book that some of the children are already familiar with. They may have heard it at home or seen a version on television or the movies.

- Don't start a book unless you have enough time to read more than a few pages.

- Don't be fooled by awards. Just because a book has received a national book award does not mean that it is suitable for your particular group of children.

- Don't impose your own interpretations or reactions to the story on the children or quiz them to see what they got out of it. Let them express their own understanding and feelings.

GREAT BOOKS TO USE WITH BABIES

Good books for infants are

- sturdy board or vinyl, which is easily cleaned after mouthing.

- illustrated with large, colorful pictures, one per page.

- relevant to infant's life experiences.

- respectful representations of diverse cultural groups.

- filled with familiar words and phrases, rich language, rhyming words, and repetition.

Look for board books by various authors as listed here.

Sandra Boynton

- ■ *Barnyard Dance.* Workman Publishers, 1993
- ■ *Moo, Baa, LaLaLa.* Little Simon, 1982
- ■ *The Going-To-Bed Book.* Little Simon, 1982
- ■ *One, Two Three!* Workman, 1993

Mem Fox

- ■ *Time for Bed.* Red Wagon Books, 1997

Tana Hoban

- ■ *Who are They?* Harper Festival, 1994
- ■ *Black on White.* Greenwillow, 1993
- ■ *Red, Blue, Yellow Shoe.* Harper Festival, 1994
- ■ *Construction Zone Board Book.* Greenwillow, 1999
- ■ *What is It?* Greenwillow, 1994

Dr. Seuss

- ■ *Hand, Hand, Fingers, Thumb,* by Al Perkins. Random House, 1969
- ■ *Mr. Brown Can Moo, Can You?* Random House, 1996

Nancy Shaw

- ■ *Sheep in a Jeep.* Houghton Mifflin, 1997

Helen Oxenbury

- ■ *Family.* Little Simon, 1981
- ■ *Friends.* Wanderer Books, 1981
- ■ *All Fall Down.* Little Simon, 1999
- ■ *Clap Hands.* Little Simon, 1999

Margaret W. Brown

- ■ *Goodnight Moon.* Harper Festival Boardbooks, 1991

Rosemary Wells

- *Goodnight Max*. Viking books, 2000
- *Max's Birthday*. Viking Books, 2004

Joy Cowley

- *Mrs. Wishy-Washy*. Philomel, 1999

Eric Carle

- *1-2-3 to the Zoo*. Philomel, 1996
- *The Very Hungry Caterpillar*. Hamish Hamilton Children's Books, 1994
- *Head to Toe*. Harper Festival, 1999

Karen Katz

- *Counting Kisses*. Little Simon, 2000
- *Where is Baby's Mommy?* Little Simon, 2001
- *Daddy and Me*. Little Simon, 2003

Marion Bauer

- *Toes, Ears, Nose*. Little Simon, 2003

Dorothy Kunhardt

- *Pat the Bunny*. Golden Books, Reissue, 2001

R. Intrater

- *Baby Faces Board Books: Eat! Splash! Smile!* See also Spanish books

I. Opia, Ed., R. Wells, Illustrator

- *My Very First Mother Goose*. Candlewick, 1996. *Note:* Do use Mother Goose—find a well-illustrated book, as you will use it for years. Each rhyme is a mini-story, complete with rhyme and rhythm.

BOOKS IN SPANISH FOR BABIES

T. Courtin

- *Bebes Dinamicos*. (Dynamic Babies) Mega Ediciones,
- *Bebes Juguetones* (Playful Babies) Mega Ediciones,

L. Cousins

- *A Maisy le gusta jugar* (Maisy Driving). Ediciones Serres,
- *A Maisy le gusta conducir* (Maisy playing), and other Maisy books. Ediciones Serres,
- *El tren de Maisy.* Ediciones Serres,
- *El coche de bomberos de Maisy.* Ediciones Serres,

S. Rotraut

- *Buenas noches* (Good night) and *Buenos dias!* (Good morning).

R. Intrater

- *Sonrie!* (Smile!).

FAVORITE BOOKS FOR TODDLERS

- Ahlberg, J. *Peek-a-Boo!* Viking, 1997
- Alexander, M. *Maggie's Moon.* Dial, 1982
- Aliki. *Hush Little Baby.* Aladdin, 1972
- Bang, M. *Ten, Nine, Eight.* Greenwillow, 1996
- Barton, B. *Airplanes.* Harper Collins, 1986
- Bruna, D. *Miffy at the Zoo.* Big Tent Entertainment, 2004
- Burningham, J. *The Baby.* Ty Crowell Co., 1976
- Campbell, R. *Dear Zoo.* Little Simon, 1986
- Carle, E. *The Very Busy Spider.* Philomel, 1984
- Carlstrom, N. *Jesse Bear, What Will You Wear?* Aladdin, 1996
- Crews, D. *Ten Black Dots.* Harper Trophy, 1995
- DePaola, T. *Tomie De Paola's Mother Goose.* Putnam, 1983
- Emberley, E. *Go Away, Big Green Monster.* Cartwheel, 1997
- Fisher, A. *Do Bears Have Mothers Too?* Crowell, 1973
- Galdone, P. *Little Bo-Peep.* Houghton Mifflin, 1986
- Gibbons, G. *Trucks.* Trophy Press, 1983
- Hill, E. *Spot's First Walk.* Putnam, 1981

- Hoban, T. *A Children's Zoo*. Greenwillow, 1985
- Howard, J. *When I'm Sleepy*. Puffin, 2001
- Hutchins, P. *Titch*. Aladdin, 1993
- Komori, A. *Animal Mothers*. Philomel, 1983
- Krauss, R. *The Carrot Seed*. HarperTrophy, 1989
- McMillan, B. *Kitten Can*. Lothrop, Lee, and Shepherd, 1984
- Mack. S. *Ten Bears in My Bed*. Knopf, 1974
- Maris, R. *Is Anyone Home?* Two-Can Publishers, 2000
- Martin, B. *Brown Bear, Brown Bear*. Henry Holt and Co., 1996
- Miller, J. *Farm Counting Book*. Little Simon, 1992
- Peek, M. *Mary Wore a Red Dress and Henry Wore His Green Sneakers*. Clarion Books, 1988
- Peppe, R. *Circus Numbers*. Longmans Young, 1969
- Rockwell, A. *Big Wheels*. Walker Books, 2003
- Rojankovsky, F. *Animals on the Farm*. Knopf, 1967
- Royo, R. *Three Ducks Went Wandering*. Clarion Books, 1987
- Speier, P. *Gobble, Growl, Grunt*. Doubleday, 1971
- Titherington, J. *Pumpkin, Pumpkin*. HarperTrophy, 1990
- Watanabe, S. *How Do I Put It On?* Philomel, 1980
- Wheeler, C. *A Good Day, A Good Night*. HarperCollins, 1980
- Wildsmith, B. *Animal Homes*. Oxford University Press, 1981
- Williams, G. *The Chicken Book*. Yearling, 1992

FAVORITE BOOKS FOR PRESCHOOLERS

Look for these and others by the same authors. The reference book *A to Zoo: Subject Access to Children's Picture Books* by Carolyn Lima will be helpful in finding more ideas, as will a listing for Caldecott award books.

- Aareema, V. *Why Mosquitoes Buzz in People's Ears: A West African Folktale*. Puffin Books, 1978
- Allen, P. *Who Sank the Boat?* Putnam Publishing Group, reissued, 1996

- Asch, F. *Bear Shadow.* Silver Burdett Printers, reprint, 1996
- Ashley, B. *Cleversticks.* Dragonfly Books, 1995
- Brett, J. *Annie and the Wild Animals.* Houghton Mifflin, 1983
- Burningham, J. *Mr. Gumpy's Outing.* Henry Holt, 1971
- Carle, E. *Mister Seahorse.* Philomel, 2004
- Crews, D. *Shortcut.* HarperTrophy, 1996
- Dabcovich, L. *Busy Beavers.* Dutton Children's Books, 1988
- DePaolo, T. *The Cloud Book.* Holiday House, 1975
- De Regneirs, B. *May I Bring a Friend?* Atheneum, 1971
- Eastman, P.D. *Are You My Mother?* Random House, 1960
- Ets, M. H. *Gilberto and the Wind.* Puffin Books, 1978
- Falconer, I. *Olivia.* Atheneum, 2000
- Feiffer, J. *Bark George.* Harper Collins, 1999
- Fleming, D. *In the Tall, Tall Grass.* Henry Holt and Co., reprint, 1995
- Fox, M. *Shoes from Grandpa.* Orchard Books, 1992
- Freeman, D. *Dandelion.* Puffin Books, 1977
- Galdone, P (illus). *Three Blind Mice.* Trumpet Club, 1987
- Gray, L. M. *Miss Tizzy.* Aladdin, 1998
- Henkes, K. *Chrysanthemum.* Harper Trophy, 1996
- Hest, A. *In the Rain with Baby Duck.* Candlewick, 1999
- Hoban, R. *Bread and Jam for Frances.* HarperCollins, 1993
- Hoberman, M. A. *A House Is a House for Me.* Puffin Books, 1982
- Hoffman, M. *Amazing Grace.* Dial, 1991
- Howard, E. *Aunt Flossie's Hats (and Crab Cakes Later).* Clarion Books, 1995
- Hutchins, P. *The Doorbell Rang.* HarperTrophy, 1989
- Keats, E. J. *Whistle for Willie.* Puffin Books, 1977
- Kimmel, E. *Anansi and the Moss-Covered Rock.* Holiday House, 1988

- Kraus, R. *Leo the Late Bloomer.* HarperTrophy, 1994

- Lobel, A. *Frog and Toad Are Friends.* HarperTrophy, 1979

- Marshall, J. *George and Martha.* Houghton Mifflin, 1997

- McCloskey, R. *Blueberries for Sal.* Viking Publishers, 1948

- McPhail, D. *Pigs Aplenty, Pigs Galore.* Puffin Books, 1996

- Numeroff, L. *If you give a Mouse a Cookie.* Laura Geringer, 1985

- Rice, E. *Benny Bakes a Cake.* Greenwillow, 1998

- Sendak, M. *Where the Wild Things Are.* HarperCollins, 1988

- Shaw, R. *It Looked Like Spilt Milk.* HarperTrophy, 1988

- Slobodkina, E. *Caps for Sale.* HarperTrophy reissue, 1987

- Tafuri, N. *Who's counting?* Greenwillow, 1986

- Yolen, J. *Owl Moon.* Philomel, 1987

GOOD BOOKS FOR PRIMARY AGED

Look for other books by these same authors.

- Blume, J. *The One in the Middle is the Green Kangaroo.* Yearling, 1982

- Bonsall, C. *The Case of the Hungry Stranger.* HarperCollins, 1992

- Brown, M. *Arthur's Tooth.* Marc Brown, 1986

- Carle, E. *The Secret Birthday Message.* HarperTrophy, 1986

- Crews, N. *One Hot Summer Day.* Greenwillow, 1995

- Dr. Seuss. *One Fish Two Fish Red Fish Blue Fish.* Random House, 1960

- Eastman, P.D. *Are You My Mother?* Random House, 1960

- Hoban, R. *A Bargain for Frances.* HarperTrophy, 1992

- Hoff, S. *Sammy the Seal.* HarperTrophy, 2000

- Kessler, L. *Kick, Pass, and Run.* HarperTrophy, 1996

- Lobel, A. *Frog and Toad All Year.* HarperTrophy, 1984

- Parrish, P. *Amelia Bedelia.* HarperTrophy, 1992

- Riley, L. *Elephants Swim.* Houghton Mifflin, 1998

- Rockwell, T. *How to Eat Fried Worms*. Yearling, 1953

- Rylant, C. *Henry and the Mudge: Puddle Trouble*. Aladdin, 1999

- Sharmat, M. *Nate the Great*. Yearling, 1977

- Skofield, J. *Detective Dinosaur*. HarperTrophy, 1998

CHAPTER BOOKS, OR BOOKS TO READ TO PRIMARY AGED. SOME ARE PART OF SERIES

- Abbott, T. *Secrets of Droon: The Hidden Stairs and Magic Carpet*. Scholastic, 1999

- Banks, L. *The Indian in the Cupboard*. HarperTrophy, 1982

- Bunting, E. *How Many Days to America?* Clarion Books, 1990

- Cameron, A. *The Stories Julian Tells*. Yearling, 1989

- Cleary, B. *Ramona Quimby Age 8*. HarperTrophy, 1992

- Dahl, R. *Charlie and the Chocolate Factory*. Puffin Books, 1998

- Danziga, P. *Amber Brown Is Not a Crayon*. Scholastic, 1995

- DiTerlizzaSpiderwick, T. *Chronicles: Book 1 Field Guide*. Simon and Schuster, 2003

- Grahame, K. *The Wind in the Willows*. Aladdin, 1989

- Jukes, M. *Like Jake and Me*. Dragonfly Books, 1987

- Kipling, R. *The Jungle Book*. Tor Books, 1992

- L'Engel, M. *A Wrinkle in Time*. Yearling, 1973

- Levine, G. *Ella Enchanted*. HarperTrophy, 1998

- Lindgren, A. *Pippi Longstocking*. Puffin, 1997

- McDonald, M. *Judy Moody*. Candlewick, 2002

- Osborne, M. *Magic Tree House: Dinosaurs Before Dark*. Random House, 1992

- Sczieska, J. *Time-Warp Trio: Knights of the Kitchen Table*. Viking, 1991

- Steig, W. *Abel's Island*. Farrar, Straus, and Giroux, 1985

- Warner, G. *Boxcar Children*. Albert Whitman and Co., 1989

- White, E. B.*Charlotte's Web*. HarperTrophy, 1974

DEVELOPMENTALLY APPROPRIATE PRACTICE

NAEYC's first position statement on developmentally appropriate practice had two main motivations:

- The process of accrediting centers required widely accepted and specific definitions of what constituted excellent practices in early childhood education.

- A proliferation of programs had inappropriate practices and expectations for their children, largely based on premature academic learning.

The original position statement did enhance the early childhood profession, although it was not received with universal acceptance, so a revised position statement clarified some of the previous misunderstandings and expanded the vision of good practices.

It is important to keep the principles firmly in mind when making professional decisions and to use the statement in conversations with others regarding appropriate practices. Colleagues, administrators, and family members all have their individual understandings of what to do with young children. Therefore, every teacher should have a copy of the position statement. In a conversation, you can use the position statement to replace the idea of personal opinions with the weight of the professional body of knowledge. The complete statement, "Developmentally Appropriate Practice in Early Childhood Programs, Revised Edition" (1997, NAEYC), can be found at http://www.naeyc.org. Click on Information About NAEYC, Position Statements, and then Developmentally Appropriate Practice. The introduction to the statement follows.

DEVELOPMENTALLY APPROPRIATE PRACTICE IN EARLY CHILDHOOD PROGRAMS SERVING CHILDREN FROM BIRTH THROUGH AGE 8

A Position Statement for the National Association for the Education of Young Children Adopted July 1996

This statement defines and describes principles of developmentally appropriate practice in early childhood programs for administrators, teachers, parents, policy-makers, and others who make decisions about the care and education of young children. An early childhood program is any group program in a center, school, or other facility that serves children from birth through age eight. Early childhood programs include childcare centers, family childcare homes, private and public preschools, kindergartens, and primary-grade schools.

- The early childhood profession is responsible for establishing and promoting standards of high-quality, professional practice in early childhood programs. These standards must reflect current knowledge and shared beliefs about what constitutes high-quality, developmentally appropriate early childhood education in the context within which services are delivered.

GUIDELINES FOR DEVELOPMENTALLY APPROPRIATE PRACTICE

NAEYC's DAP guidelines can be implemented in your daily work with children.

- Create a Caring Environment among Children and Adults
  Children
    - learn personal responsibility.
    - develop constructive relationships with others.
    - respect individual and cultural difference.
  Adults
    - get to know each child, taking into account individual differences and developmental levels.
    - adjust the pace and content of the curriculum so that children can be successful most of the time.
    - bring each child's culture and language into the setting, welcoming their families.
    - expect children to be tolerant of others' differences.

- The Curriculum and Schedule Allow Children to Select and Initiate Their Own Activities
  Children
    - learn through active involvement in a variety of learning experiences.
    - build independence by taking on increasing responsibilities.
    - initiate their own activities to follow their interests.
  Adults
    - provide a variety of materials and activities that are concrete and real.
    - provide a variety of work places and spaces.

- arrange the environment so that children can work alone or in groups.
- extend children's learning by posing problems and asking thought-provoking questions.
- add complexity to tasks as needed.
- model, demonstrate, and provide information so children can progress in their learning.

■ **The Program Is Organized and Integrated So that Children Develop a Deeper Understanding of Key Concepts and Skills**
Children
- engage in activities that reflect their current interests.
- plan and predict outcomes of their research.
- share information and knowledge with others.

Adults
- plan related activities and experiences that broaden children's knowledge and skills.
- design curriculum to foster important skills such as literacy and numeracy.
- adapt instruction for children who are ahead or behind age-appropriate expectations.
- plan curriculum so that children achieve important developmental goals.

■ **Activities and Experiences Help Children Develop a Positive Self-Image within a Democratic Community**
Children
- learn through reading books about other cultures.
- read about current events and discuss how these relate to different cultures.
- accept differences among their peers, including children with disabilities.

Adults
- provide culturally and nonsexist activities and materials that foster children's self-identity.
- design the learning environment so children can learn new skills while using their native language.
- allow children to demonstrate their learning using their own language.
- facilitate discussion and problem-solving among children.

■ Activities and Experiences Develop Children's Awareness of the Importance of Community Involvement

Children

- are ready and eager to learn about the world outside their immediate environment.
- are open to considering different ways of thinking or doing things.
- can benefit from contact with others outside their homes or childcare setting.

Adults

- encourage awareness of the community at large, as well as a sense of the classroom community.
- plan experiences in facilities within the community.
- bring outside resources and volunteers into the childcare setting.
- encourage children to plan their involvement based on their own interests.

PROFESSIONAL ORGANIZATIONS

When looking to further your development, a professional organization is a great place to start. Several organizations exist, some of which even have state or local affiliates.

National Association for the Education of Young Children (NAEYC)
1509 16th Street, NW
Washington DC 20036
Phone: 800-424-2460
Web site: http://www.naeyc.org
Email: membership@naeyc.org

Comprehensive Members receive

- all the benefits of Regular membership described next.
- five or six books annually immediately after their release by NAEYC.

Regular and Student Members receive

- six issues of *Young Children,* which includes timely articles on pertinent issues, as well as suggestions and strategies for enhancing children's learning.
- reduced registration fees at NAEYC-sponsored local and national conferences and seminars.
- discounted prices on hundreds of books, videos, brochures, and posters from NAEYC's extensive catalog of materials.
- access to the Members Only Web site, including links to additional resources and chat sites for communication with other professionals.

National Association of Child Care Professionals (NACCP)
P.O. Box 90723
Austin, TX 78709
Phone: 800-537-1118
Web site: http://www.naccp.org

Specific membership benefits:

- Complete and free access (a $79 value) to the effective **Management Tools of the Trade**, which provide technical assistance in human resource management.

- NACCP's three quarterly trade journals, ***Professional Connections, Teamwork, and Caring for Your Children***, to help you stay on top of hot issues in childcare. Each edition also includes a Tool of the Trade.

National Child Care Association (NCCA)
1016 Rosser St.
Conyers GA 30012
Phone: 800-543-7161
Web site: http://www.nccanet.org

Specific membership benefits:

- As the only recognized voice in Washington DC, NCCA has great influence on legislators.

- Professional development opportunities are available.

Association for Education International (ACEI)
The Olney Professional Building
17904 Georgia Avenue, Suite 215
Olney, MD 20832
Phone: 800-423-2563 or 301-570-2122
Fax: 301-570-2212
Web site: http://www.acei.org

ACEI is an international organization dedicated to promoting the best educational practices throughout the world.

Specific membership benefits:

- Workshops and travel/study tours abroad

- Four issues per year of the journal *Childhood Education* and the *Journal of Research in Childhood Education*

- Hundreds of resources for parents and teachers, including books, pamphlets, audiotapes, and videotapes

National AfterSchool Association (NAA)
1137 Washington Street
Boston, MA 02124
Phone: 617-298-5012
Fax: 617-298-5022
Web site: http://www.naaweb.org

NAA is a national organization dedicated to providing information, technical assistance, and resources concerning children in out-of-school programs. Members include teachers, policy-makers, and administrators representing all public, private, and community-based sectors of after-school programs.

Specific member benefits:
- A subscription to the NAA journal, *School-Age Review*
- A companion membership in state affiliates
- Discounts on NAA publications and products
- Discount on NAA annual conference registration
- Opportunity to be an NAA accreditation endorser
- Public policy representatives in Washington, DC

OTHER ORGANIZATIONS TO CONTACT:

The Children's Defense Fund
25 E. St. NW
Washington DC 20001
Phone: 202-628-8787
Web site: http://www.childrensdefense.org

National Association for Family Child Care
P.O. Box 10373
Des Moines, IA 50306
Phone: 800-359-3817
Web site: http://www.nafcc.org
Journal: *The National Perspective*

National Black Child Development Institute
1023 15th Ave. NW
Washington DC 20002
Phone: 202-833-2220
Web site: http://www.nbcdi.org

National Head Start Association
1651 Prince Street
Alexandria VA 22314

Phone: 703-739-0875
Web site: http://www.nhsa.org
Journal: *Children and Families*

International Society for the Prevention of Child Abuse and Neglect
25 W. 560 Geneva Road, Suite L2C
Carol Stream, IL 60188
Phone: 630-221-1311
Web site: http://www.ispcan.org
Journal: *Child Abuse and Neglect: The International Journal*

Council for Exceptional Children
1110N. Glebe Road, Suite 300,
Arlington, VA 22201
Phone: 888-CEC-SPED
Web site: http://www.cec.sped.org
Journal: *CEC Today*

National Association for Bilingual Education
Union Center Plaza
810 First Street, NE
Washington DC 20002
Phone: 202-898-1829
Web site: http://www.nabe.org
Journal: *NABE Journal of Research and Practice*

International Reading Association
800 Barksdale Road
P.O. Box 8139
Newark, DE 19714
Phone: 800-336-READ
Web site: http://www.reading.org
Journal: *The Reading Teacher*

National Education Organization (NEA)
1201 16th St. NW
Washington, DC 20036
Phone: 202-833-4000
Web site: http://www.nea.org
Journals: *Works4Me* and *NEA Focus,* by online subscription

Zero to Three: National Center for Infants, Toddlers, and Families
2000M. Street NW, Suite 200
Washington DC 20036
Phone: 202-638-1144
Web site: http://www.zerotothree.org
Journal: *Zero to Three*

RESOURCES

BOOKS

Berk, L., & Winsler, A. (1995). *Scaffolding children's learning: Vygotsky and early childhood education*. Washington, DC: NAEYC.

Curtis, D., & Carter, M. (1996). *Reflecting children's lives: A handbook for planning child-centered curriculum*. St. Paul, MN: Redleaf Press.

Curtis, D., & Carter, M. (2000). *The Art of Awareness: How Observation Can Transform Your Teaching*. St. Paul, MN: Redleaf Press.

Dodge, D., Colker, L.,& Heroman, C. (2002). *The Creative Curriculum for Preschool*. (4th ed.). Washington, DC: Teaching Strategies, Inc.

Engel, B., & Gronlund, G. (2001). *Focused Portfolios: A complete assessment for the young child*. St. Paul, MN: Redleaf Press.

Edwards, C., Gandini, L., & Forman, G. (Eds.). (1998). *The hundred languages of children: The Reggio Emilia approach to education*. (2nd ed.). Norwood, NJ: Ablex.

Gestwicki, C. (2004). *Home, School, Community Relations: A guide to working with families*. Clifton Park, NY: Thomson Delmar Learning.

Gould, P., Sullivan, J., & Waites, J. (1999). *The Inclusive Early Childhood Classroom: Easy Ways to Adapt Learning Centers for all Children*. Beltsville, MD: Gryphon House Inc.

Helm, J., & Katz, L. (2001). *Young Investigators: The Project Approach in the Early Years*. New York: Teachers College Press.

Hohmann, M., & Weikart, D. (2002). *Educating Young Children: Active Learning Practices for Preschool and Child Care Programs.* (2nd ed.). Ypsilanti, MI: High/Scope Press.

Jones, E., Evans, K., & Rencken, K. (2001). *The Lively Kindergarten: Emergent Curriculum in Action.* Washington, DC: NAEYC.

Jones, E., & Nimmo, J. (1994). *Emergent curriculum.* Washington, DC: NAEYC.

Jones, E., & Reynolds, G. (1992). *The play's the thing: Teachers' roles in children's play.* New York: Teachers' College Press.

Katz, L., & Chard, S. (2000). *Engaging children's minds: The project approach.* (2nd ed.). Norwood, NJ: Ablex.

Klein, M.D., Cook, R., & Richardson-Gibbs, A.M. (2000). *Strategies for Including Children with Special Needs in Early Childhood Settings.* Clifton Park, NY: Thomson Delmar Learning.

Owocki, G. (1999) *Literacy Through Play.* Portsmouth, NH: Heinemann.

Paley, V. (2004). *A Child's Work: The Importance of Fantasy Play.* Chicago: University of Chicago Press.

Schickedanz, J., & R. Casbergue. (2005). *Writing in Preschool: Learning to orchestrate meaning and marks.* Washington, DC: International Reading Assoc.

Schwartz, I., & Sandall, S. (2002). *Building Blocks for Teaching Preschoolers with Special Needs.* Baltimore, MD: Paul. H. Brookes Pub. Co.

Wasserman, S. (2000). *Serious players in the primary classroom: Empowering children through active learning experiences.* (2nd ed.). New York:.

Zigler, E., Singer, D., & Bishop-Josef, S. (Eds.). (2004). *Children's Play: The roots of reading.* Washington, DC: Zero to Three Press.

INTERNET RESOURCES

http://www.acei.org
The Association for Childhood Education International Web site has the latest position statements of the organization regarding guidelines for early childhood education. Click on Professional Standards to find "Global Guidelines for Early Childhood Education and Care

in the Twenty-first Century" (2002), and an individual checklist for self-assessment on the standards. You can also download a copy of the ACEI brochure "Play's Role in Brain Development."

http://www.naeyc.org
The National Association for the Education of Young Children Web site has all the position statements on developmentally appropriate practice and early childhood curriculum and assessment, as well as the statements on appropriate teaching of mathematics and literacy. Click on Resources, and then on Position Statements. Following are the statements currently listed. New ones are added from time to time.

Accreditation criteria

- Anti-Discrimination statements
- Code of Ethical Conduct and Statement of Commitment
- El Codigo de Conducta Etica y Declaracion de Compriso
- Developmentally Appropriate Practice
- Developing and Implementing Policies to Promote Accreditation
- Early Childhood Curriculum, Assessment, and Program Evaluation Where We Stand Summary
- Complete Position Statement with Expanded Resources
- Early Childhood Mathematics Promoting Good Beginnings
- Summary
- Complete Statement
- Early Learning Standards
- Guiding Principles for Development and Analysis of Early Childhood Public Policy
  - Inclusion
- Learning to Read and Write
- Licensing and Public Regulation
- Media Violence in Children's Lives
- Prevention of Child Abuse
- Where We Stand Summary

- Quality, Compensation, and Affordability
- Responding to Linguistic and Cultural Diversity
- Where We Stand Summary
- Respuesta a la Diversidad Linguistica y Cultural
- School Readiness
- Where We Stand Summary
- Standards for Professional Preparation Programs
  - Where We Stand Summary
  - Initial Licensure Programs
  - Advanced Degree Programs
  - Associate Degree Programs
- Still Unacceptable Trends in Kindergarten Entry and Placement
- Technology and Young Children
- Violence in the Lives of Children

http://www.famlit.org
The National Center for Family Literacy Web site has much information on literacy.

http://www.highscope.org
The High/Scope Educational Research Foundation Web site has much information about the philosophy and resources for learning more about the High/Scope Curriculum.

http://www.teachingstrategies.com
The Creative Curriculum Web site has much information about all aspects of this curriculum approach and resources.

http://www.reggioalliance.org
The North American Reggio Emilia Alliance (NAREA) Web site has much information about what educators are doing in their explorations of the Reggio approach.

http://www.reggiochildren.it
The official Web site for Reggio children has information in both English and Italian.

http://www.eceWebguide.com
The ECE Web Guide Web site is an invaluable resource on many topics.

http://ceep.crc.uiuc.edu
This Web site is the archive of ERIC/EECE Digests. Search here for several articles on developmentally appropriate practice.

http://www.instituteforplay.com
The Importance of Play Web site has much information about play.

http://www.project-approach.com
Formerly at the University of Alberta Web site, the project approach Web site has much information about this approach to curriculum.

http://www.zerotothree.org
On the Zero to Three Web site, there is a great deal of information about the care and education of infants and toddlers.

http://www.niost.org
The National Institute on Out-of-School Time Web site, sponsored by Wellesley College has much information about curriculum and environments for after-school programs.

http://www.schoolagenotes.com
This Web site has much information on setting up appropriate environments and schedules in after-school programs.

http://www.scholastic.com
On this Web site, search for a number of articles on children's social and emotional development.

http://www.nncc.org
The National Network for Child Care Web site has a number of helpful articles on topics related to childcare.

http://www.kidshealth.org
The Kids Health Web site has a number of helpful articles on healthy development.

http://www.tolerance.org
The Teaching Tolerance Web site has much information and resources for teachers who want to implement anti-bias practices in their classrooms.

http://www.childrensbookabout.com

This Web site has much information about children's books. Search under Tolerance/Racism/prejudice for the article by the Council for Interracial Children's Books about evaluating children's books for racism.

http://www.nccic.org

The National Child Care Information Center Web site, run by the US Department of Health and Human Services, Administration for Children and Families, has information and helpful links.

http://www.aap.org

The American Academy of Pediatrics Web site has much information. For the position statement on "Television and How It Affects Children," click on Health Topics, and then to topics for Television.

http://www.kidsource.com

This Web site has many articles about children's education and health.

http://www.reading.org

The International Reading Organization Web site has much information, including several position statements such as "Using Multiple Methods of Beginning Reading Instruction" (1998).

http://www.rif.org

The Reading is Fundamental Web site has much information for teachers and parents about helpful literacy practices.

http://www.picturebookart.org

The Eric Carle Museum of Picture Book Art Web site includes valuable information about children's books. Click on Education, then on Recommended books to find several lists, including Best Picture Books for 2001, 2002, and 2003, and bibliographies of particular topics such as: moving day; African American literature; men in picture Books; Jewish folk tales in contemporary picture books; Chinese tales in picture books, and many more.

http://www.ala.org

The American Library Association Web site has many reading resources. Click Libraries and You, and then Recommended Reading. You will find resources for children, including 2005 Notable Children's Books; Caldecott Medal and Honor books; Coretta Scott King Award and Honor books; Newberry Medal and Honor books; and more recommended book lists from The Association of Library Services to Children (ALSC), such as books dealing with diversity, bilingual books for children, and many more.

http://www.teachingbooks.com
This Web site has thematic book lists, as well as discussion guides for thousands of books.

http://www.umaine.edu/eceol
The Early Childhood Education Online Web site offers support and opportunities for information exchange, as well as a listserv discussion, for all educators and parents serving children from birth through age eight.

http://www.forums.atozteacherstuff.com
This Web site has much information, as well as forums for discussion for educators.

http://www.edpsych.com
The Early Childhood Educators Web site offers information and opportunities for discussion.

http://www.sitesforteachers.com
Hundreds of educational Web sites are summarized and rated. This site also includes a lot of free stuff.

http://www.assortedstuff.com
The top 100 Web sites for teachers.

http://www.edweb.sdsu.edu
Clink on links for connections to many teacher Web sites, with resources and curriculum plans.

VIDEOS FOR CAREGIVERS

Developmentally Appropriate Practice: Birth through Age 5.

(27 minutes)

Based on the position statement, this video includes both appropriate and inappropriate practices, #854, NAEYC, (800) 424-2460.

Space to Grow: Creating a Child Care Environment for Infants and Toddlers

(22 minutes)

California Department of Education/WestEd, Bureau of Publications Sales Unit, (800) 995-4099.

Time with Toddlers

(22 minutes)

Margie Carter and Kidspace, a consideration of toddler development, typical toddler behaviors, and recommended caregiver actions. Distributed by Redleaf Press, (800) 423-8309.

Space to Grow: How the environment supports language and learning

(30 minutes)

A consideration of appropriate environments for preschoolers. Educational Productions, (800) 950-4949.

A Place of their Own: Designing Quality Space for Out of School Time

(15 minutes)

Appropriate environments for after-school care. NIOST, part of Wellesley Centers for Work at Wellesley College, (781) 283-2547.

Setting the Stage for School Aged Care

(30 minutes)

Another good resource on environments for after-school care. Insight Media, (800) 233-9910.

It's Mine: Responding to Problems and Conflict

(40 minutes)

Working with conflict among the youngest children. Tender Care Infant-toddler Video Series, available from High/Scope Press, (734) 485-2000.

Supporting Children in Resolving Conflicts

(30 minutes)

Shows teachers working with preschoolers how to help teach conflict resolution skills. High/Scope Press, see above.

Children and Conflict: An Opportunity for Learning in the Early Childhood Classroom

(15 minutes)

More good principles of conflict resolution. NAEYC, see above.

Learning from Others: Learning in a Social Context

(30 minutes)

Explores ways teachers can support cooperative learning in primary classrooms. Insight Media, see above.

Scaffolding Self-Regulated Learning in the Primary Grades

(34 minutes)

Explores teacher support of active learning in primary grades. Davidson Films, (888) 437-4200.

Performance Assessment: A Teacher's Way of Knowing, with Samuel Meisels

(21 minutes)

Describes assessment by children's performance, by the person who developed one system. Davidson, see above.

Creating Literacy Environments in the Classroom

(minutes)

Ideas about how to use the environment to promote literacy. Insight Media, see above.

Plan-Do-Review in the High/Scope Demonstration Preschool

Set of three videos (63 minutes)

A good introduction to the way High/Scope looks in a preschool classroom. High/Scope, see above.

The Creative Curriculum Video

(37 minutes)

An overview of the Creative Curriculum approach in preschool classrooms. Available from Teaching Strategies, Inc., (202) 362-7543, or from Redleaf Press, see above.

To Make a Portrait of a Lion

(32 minutes)

A record of an extended project in a Reggio Emilia preschool. Learning Materials Workshop, (800) 693-7164.

Children at the Center: Reflective Teachers at Work

(24 minutes)

Shows teachers dialogue as they try to develop curriculum based on their observations of children. Harvest Resources, (206) 325-0592, or Redleaf Press, as above.

Setting Sail: An Emergent Curriculum Project

(19 minutes)

Demonstrates an emergent curriculum project, from beginning to end. Harvest Resources and Redleaf Press, as above.

Thinking Big: Extending Emergent Curriculum Projects

(22 minutes)

Shows two teachers working to deepen children's learning through active exploration. Harvest Resources and Redleaf Press, as above.

To See Takes Time: Growing Curriculum from Children's Theories

Another exploration of curriculum that emerges from children's ideas and interests. Harvest Resources and Redleaf Press, as above.

Involving Families in Active Learning Settings

(23 minutes)

Demonstrates how to involve families in preschool programs. High/Scope, see above.

Teachers have decisions to make every day as they encounter specific situations. There is no one right answer in any situation. Usually some ideas are more helpful and appropriate than others. In the process of decision-making, teachers have to consider their knowledge of child development and children's needs and their understanding of their professional responsibilities. They also have to articulate and explain to others their reasons for the decisions they make. Thinking about hypothetical case studies is useful practice in considering the questions of what is most helpful. Consider these situations and reflect on what you would do and why. Then ask yourself the same questions to guide your decision-making the next time you are puzzled by a decision in your particular setting.

1. A teacher of toddlers is faced with parents who insist that their children should really be learning something. By this, they mean academics, such as alphabets, phonics, and math. She is struggling to reconcile her knowledge of developmentally appropriate practice and active learning, and these demands. What would you do?

   What knowledge would you consider? What approaches could you take? What do you believe would be the wrong response?

2. A first-grade teacher has been trying to move away from basal readers and workbooks in her classroom. Her problem is that the parents have been getting upset when the work they see is mostly drawings, with a few letters and difficult to decipher words on it. They are concerned that their children will not be prepared to pass the end-of-grade tests coming in the future at the end of third grade. She is concerned about how best to convince them that their children are learning. What would you do?

What knowledge would you consider? What approaches could you take? What do you believe would be the wrong response?

3. A teacher is worried about the parent of a child in her toddler class who demands to know who bit her child yesterday. She knows the parent is upset and is concerned about what the parent's response would be if she knew it was the same child who scratched her child last week. What would you do?

What knowledge would you consider? What approaches could you take? What do you believe would be the wrong response?

4. A mother of a five-month-old infant in your center asks the caregiver to keep the baby on a strict by-the-clock schedule so she can feed him his evening meal as soon as she gets home from work and put him right to bed, leaving her free to do household chores. The caregiver finds it difficult to keep to the schedule, because sometimes it means waking him from a nap, and other times it means he's hungry before the prescribed hour. What would you do, in this situation?

What knowledge would help you make your decision? What approach would you take? What do you believe would be the incorrect response?

5. One child in the after-school program is continually picked on by the other children. As you observe, you realize that he doesn't seem to understand how to play some of the games or how to communicate as easily as do most of the other children. What do you believe is the appropriate role for the teacher in this situation?

What knowledge would help you in making your decision? What approach would you take? What do you believe would be the incorrect response?

6. A parent tells you that she doesn't want her child to participate in the class party before Christmas. The child is one of the quietest children in your group with few friends. You're concerned about how this will affect her social relationships if she does not participate. You've always had a Christmas party and are not sure how the other children

would react if you don't have it this year. What are some possibilities for you to solve this situation? What will be your most important considerations? How will you communicate your decision, and to whom?

7. Your principal tells you that she wants to remove recess from the schedule for your first graders. She states that they need all the time for concentrating on their academic subjects. You don't believe this is in the best interests of the children. What will you do? What will you communicate, and with whom? Why do you believe this is the best decision?

ISSUES AND TRENDS

CODE OF ETHICS

One of the hallmarks of a profession is the adherence to a code of ethics by its practitioners. The National Association for the Education of Young Children first published a Code of Ethics in 1987. A revised version is being published in 2005.

The reason a Code of Ethics is essential to a profession is so that teachers have a resource to use when faced with an ethical dilemma. Rather than using standards of individual morality in making decisions about appropriate responses, teachers can use the Code of Ethics to determine appropriate professional actions. For example, what would a teacher do if a parent demanded to know who bit her child? Or when a coworker complains about another coworker's treatment of a child? What is a teacher's responsibility when another teacher tells of symptoms that make her suspicious of child abuse, but she is afraid to report? These are all situations where the right answer may carry an element of risk, such as losing a job or alienating others with whom an individual must work.

The Code consists of statements of ideals and principles for action related to four distinct groups to which teachers are responsible: to the children with whom they work, to the families they serve, to coworkers and supervisors, and to the communities in which they work. As teachers read the Code and become familiar with its ideas, they are able to make difficult decisions that go beyond their individual ideas.

One of the issues that faces early childhood professionals today is that some practitioners are still not aware that there is a

Code and try to make decisions based on what is expedient, rather than what is correct and focused on core professional values. Another problem is that the Code is a tool only, not an absolute prescription for what to do. Teachers have to use the Code to sort out conflicts between established beliefs. For example, in the issue about informing parents about biting, most good teachers believe in the importance of informing parents of issues involving their children and in maintaining lines of communication. But at the same time, they believe in protecting children's rights to privacy while they are in a center. By carefully reading the various segments of the Code, teachers are able to find the relevant ideals and principles, and decide which have priority and precedent in deciding on the most ethical course of action. Principle P.1.1 gives precedence over any other considerations to protect children.

As a beginning professional, what can you do to promote professional use of the Code of Ethics?

- Read and become thoroughly familiar with the Code. Have a copy available in your classroom.

- Promote discussion of the principles with coworkers. *Young Children* has published typical questions in past issues and has shown how to use the various parts of the Code to work through to a decision. These could be used in staff meetings or informal conversations.

- Don't take decisions lightly, or take the easy way out. Just because other teachers do something doesn't mean that it is right. Refer to the Code and consider carefully. Individual teachers have the power to help make things right for children, families, coworkers, supervisors, and for the community at large.

LITERACY

Concerns about children's success or lack of success in reading as they progress through school have brought national attention to the topic of literacy. This is actually a good thing, as laying foundations for school success has always been an important goal of early childhood education. Attention to literacy brings necessary attention to the importance of the early years.

One of the difficulties facing teachers today is that wide mis-understandings exist about what constitutes appropriate literacy education in the earliest years. Unfortunately, for some parents and even teachers, attention to literacy has been translated as beginning academic instruction in reading and phonics earlier and earlier. This leads to such inappropriate practices as two-year-olds being drilled with flash cards, and three- and four-year olds spending too much time with worksheets and pencil and paper tasks. Although these misinterpretations have led to inappropriate practices, that should not diminish the importance of providing appropriate literacy experiences for young children.

Teachers are helpful to parents when they don't react in horror, saying, "We don't teach reading and writing in the preschool." Rather, they agree, "We are laying the foundations for literacy in the preschool, and this is what it looks like. It may look differently than you expect with young children."

Appropriate literacy beginnings in the preschool include

- an awareness that literacy learning begins at birth and includes learning about oral and written language, intertwined with other learning and relationships.

- an understanding that children learn literacy just as they learn spoken language, by being immersed in it and involved with others who are using the skills.

- a philosophy that all adults in a child's life are supporting language and literacy, involving families and teachers in the ideas.

Appropriate activities and materials for literacy in the preschool include

- a lot of reading, both individually and to groups, of all kinds of good children's literature, and an inviting book area.

- materials and activities that invite conversation, such as telephones, puppets, flannelboards, small work areas, relaxed snacktimes, group time activities, and time to spend with children.

- experiences that lead to description and new vocabulary. Experiences are related to literacy understanding.

- songs, fingerplays, and other word games that help children expand their vocabulary and word understanding.

- materials to use for writing, such as paper, markers, pencils and other desk tools.

- opportunities to connect words and print, such as dictated stories, labeling, posted notes, teachers making experience charts, a print-rich environment, and making get well cards and thank you notes.

- support of children's interest in reading and writing, adding alphabet letters and words to copy on request.

- a book-lending system for families home reading.

As teachers help families understand how these developmentally appropriate introductions to literacy will be more meaningful to their children than drilling alphabets, families can become partners in literacy.

To support appropriate early literacy, teachers can

- become very familiar with the current research and position statements on literacy. Check the Web sites for family literacy, the International Reading Organization, and NAEYC for this information (found in the "Internet Resources" section earlier).

- find active alternatives when pressured to use academic approaches to literacy.

- read, read, read to the children. Their responses will show clearly how they are becoming "hooked on books"—the very best beginning to literacy.

THE NO CHILD LEFT BEHIND ACT AND ITS EFFECT ON CLASSROOMS

The No Child Left Behind Act, signed into federal law in January 2002, has widespread implications for schools and teachers all over the country. Planned to increase accountability and standards, the legislation has four key principles.

1. Stronger accountability for results.

2. Greater flexibility for states and school districts in their use of federal funds.

3. More choices for parents of children from disadvantaged backgrounds.

4. An emphasis on teaching methods that have been demonstrated to be effective.

Key provisions include

■ state standards that must be challenging, with curricula developed to align with the standards.

■ testing requirements that are expanded to include annual assessments in grades 3-8 starting in 2005-2006.

■ states participate in biennial National Assessment of Educational Programs in reading and math every other year.

To describe in more detail, states must define adequate yearly progress for districts and schools, with separate annual measurement objectives for economically disadvantaged, disabled, and LEP students, and for students from major racial and ethnic groups. States must establish a 12-year timeline to get all students to the defined "proficient" level of the state. If schools do not meet adequate yearly progress standards for 2 consecutive years, the district must provide all students an option to transfer to another public school in the district. If they do not meet adequate yearly progress for 3 years, low-income students who remain in the school must be given an option of supplemental educational programs.

New teachers in Title I schools that teach core subjects must be "highly qualified." Existing teachers must meet these standards by 2005-2006. Finally, parents must be clearly informed, in suitable language, of the school's progress and their rights for their children.

What all this means, in summary, is an enormous emphasis on meeting standards for curriculum and end-of-year test results. Although every teacher and supervisor expects to be held accountable for their performance and applauds the idea of parental choice and information, the emphasis on testing as the sole standard for schools and classrooms can create some unsound pedagogical practices. In some cases, teachers complain of being asked to use inappropriate practices and eliminate more appropriate curriculum, all in the interest of test results. Preschools are often being pressured to adopt less appropriate curricula, to prepare their young children for rigorous academics in the coming years.

The development of Early Learning Standards in most states has given direction to curriculum planning, while unfortunately seeming to assume that all children are on the same developmental timetable. It takes knowledgeable teachers and administrators to negotiate between what they know are developmentally appropriate practice and some of the pronouncements from state and federal governments.

How will this affect you as a beginning teacher, and what can you do?

■ Become very familiar with the No Child Left Behind Act and its requirements. For one thing, you may be asked to interpret some of the law to concerned families, as well as understanding what is true and what is not. You can read the whole law at http://www.nclb.org. Stay informed about changes and state challenges to the law.

■ Reflect on principles of developmentally appropriate practice, and see how some of the expectations for classroom teachers can be reconciled with the requirements of the No Child Left Behind Act.

■ Realize that teachers must take initiative to ask questions and continue dialogue with administrators and school district officials, making alliances with others who have the same concerns.

■ Become an active member of any local professional organization. Brainstorm with others on ways to comply with standards while providing authentic classroom experiences for children.

■ Demonstrate your accountability and your children's progress in learning in ways beyond test scores. It is an early childhood educator's responsibility to spread the news and widen perspectives about development of the whole child.

As teachers involve themselves with these and other current issues in the early childhood field, they take on the important role of advocate. Teachers must look beyond the classroom to focus on important long-term goals. This will contribute to your growth as a professional.

NOTES